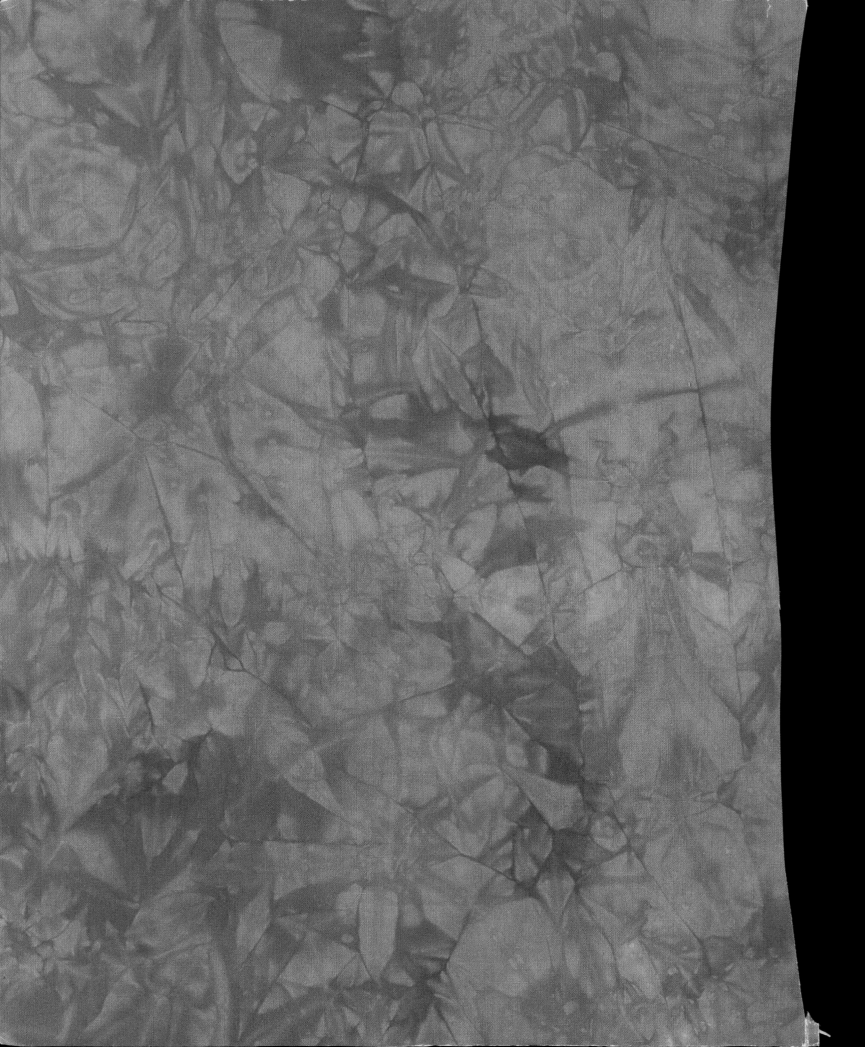

DYEING to QUILT

Quick Direct-Dye Methods for Quilt Makers

JOYCE MORI AND CYNTHIA MYERBERG

THE QUILT DIGEST PRESS
Simply the Best from NTC Publishing Group
Lincolnwood, Illinois U.S.A.

Editorial and production direction by Anne Knudsen.

Book design by John Lyle Design, San Francisco.

Cover design by Kim Bartko.

Editing by Mary Elizabeth Johnson.

Technical editing by Mary Elizabeth Johnson.

Technical drawings by Kandy Petersen.

Drawings by Julia Sharf.

Quilt photography by Sharon Risedorph, San Francisco.

Cover photograph and fabric photography by Chris Cassidy, Chicago.

Printed in Hong Kong

Library of Congress Cataloging-in-Publication Data

Mori, Joyce.

    Dyeing to Quilt : quick direct-dye methods for quilt makers / Joyce Mori and Cynthia Myerberg.

       p. cm.

    Includes bibliographical references.

    ISBN 0-8442-2626-2

    1. Dyes and dyeing—Textile fibers.   2. Dyes and dyeing, Domestic.

    3. Quilting. I Myerberg, Cynthia. II Title.

    TT853.M67   1997

    667'.3—dc20   96-33622

                                   CIP

Published by The Quilt Digest Press

a division of NTC/Contemporary Publishing Company

4255 West Touhy Avenue

Lincolnwood (Chicago), Illinois 60646-1975, U.S.A.

7 8 9 0 WKT 0 9 8 7 6 5 4 3 2 1

ACKNOWLEDGMENTS

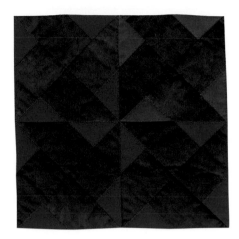

We wish to thank Delores Stemple for the beautiful hand quilting of many of the quilts in this book. Special thanks to Theresa Fleming of Aurora, CO, for machine quilting one of the quilts. Our thanks also to Anne Knudsen and all the people at The Quilt Digest Press for their tireless work in taking our manuscript and adding their creativity to make this colorful and exciting book.

FROM JOYCE

I want to thank my husband, John, for his patience while I worked on this book. He puts up with dyed fabric all over our shared studio and curing fabric in the laundry room. He helps me when I get stumped with color choices. His love and support help me through all aspects of developing and writing a book. My sincere thanks also to my good friend Pat Hill who always has so many wonderful ideas for quilts. I appreciate her willingness to share them.

FROM CYNTHIA

I would like to thank my husband, David, for his continued moral support in writing this book. Since, at the same time, I was studying for exams, planning my daughter's wedding, and making her dress, his help was invaluable. My thanks, also, to my family and friends for *ooh*-ing and *aah*-ing over my fabrics and quilts and for encouraging me to pursue the work that I love. Special thanks to my niece, Ashley Cohen, who wrote the poem *The Rainbow Maker* when she was just 11 years old, inspiring me to make the quilt on page 102. The quilt will be a gift to Ashley when she graduates high school.

CONTENTS

BRIGHT IDEAS
30" x 30" (76 cm x 76 cm)
Designed, sewn, hand-appliquéd, and hand-quilted Pat Hill, West Hills, CA
The strip-pieced background is a wonderful way to combine a wide range of scraps
of dyed fabrics. The background shades from dark to light, back to dark.

INTRODUCTION

When we walk into a fabric store or quilt shop, many of us are soon overwhelmed by the variety of fabrics, their prints, patterns, and colors. There are bolts and bolts of beautiful cottons, perfect for quilting, in every color of the rainbow. Each shop is different, reflecting the tastes of the owners and their customers. In addition to the variety from one shop to the next, there are seasonal changes in fabric selection, each new season bringing new styles, colors, and textures. If it's inspiration you're looking for, there are no better places than fabric stores and quilt shops to enjoy the sheer excitement of color and pattern to be found in fabric.

Today, hand-dyed fabrics have emerged as an important element of art quilts—those quilts intended to be viewed as works of art, most often on the wall. The first major showing of art quilts was at the first Quilt National at the Dairy Barn in Athens, Ohio in 1979. Sixteen years later, in 1995, more than half the quilts in Quilt National had some type of dyed fabric in them. As Nancy Taylor, one of the artists featured, says, "Recently I have been painting, dyeing, spraying, and using wax resist to create my own designs on fabric. . . . The balance between the aspects that I can control and the elements of surprise that are always present in theses processes is intriguing to me." (*Quilt National: Contemporary Designs in Fabric*, Lark Books, Asheville, North Carolina. 1995. p.27.)

Fortunately, for Nancy Taylor or anyone who wants to be creative, expressive, and challenged, dyeing fabric today is far less daunting than it was for the quilters of the past. Specifically, the dyes we use today are made especially for fabric. They come in a wide range of wonderful permanent bright colors, are very easy to use, and produce reliable results. Also, fabric ready for dyeing is available for purchase.

WHY SHOULD QUILTERS HAND DYE?

So why would you even consider dyeing fabrics for quilting? See if any of the following reasons strike a chord with you—if so, you may be yearning to dye.

• In spite of all the hundreds of choices in fabric and quilt shops, the color or texture you have in mind is just not there.
• You have a quilt that needs a jolt of life from a special, unique color—perhaps a special background neutral.
• There are times when you would like your quilt to be truly original, when you would like complete control of your color choices.
• You are curious about all this talk of controlling color, and you want to know more about it.
• You have made the transition from quilts as a bed-covering to quilts as art, and the fabrics you find seem too traditional for your designs.
• You want the feeling of being on the cutting edge of quilt making today.

Dyeing your own fabrics brings a new dimension to your work—the quilts you make are like no others. When you create your own colors, your choices are unlimited. You can match fabrics and prints exactly if you desire. The quilt in your mind's eye can become the quilt on your wall or bed, with no compromises. Dyeing your own fabrics opens the door to new creative challenges.

Dyeing to Quilt is a revelation for anyone who's never dyed before, and a revolutionary concept for those who have. The simplicity, flexibility, and versatility of the two basic techniques the book offers are almost unbelievable. No longer is dyeing confined to the basement or outdoors, with big buckets and large pieces of wet fabric; *Dyeing to Quilt* teaches you how to dye in a bowl or a plastic drinking cup on your kitchen counter or card table. If you can dye Easter eggs, you can dye your own fabrics—truly!

If you have always been a little nervous about dyeing, if you have thought it would be too technical and too much work, you will be reassured by the simplicity of the two methods we recommend—the bowl and cup methods. Once you've mastered the basics, you can go on to learn how to do the things with color you've always dreamed of—subtle gradations, shading, optical illusions, luminosity, transparency. The colors you can make and the variations on each are unlimited. Before you know it, you will be coloring with confidence, and will soon find that the pleasure of dyeing becomes an important part of your quilting experience.

DYEING FABRICS IS EASY—AND FAST

When you decide to dye your own fabric for quilting, you are joining a long-established tradition. Our ancestors used dyes made from plants and other natural materials. It is very possible that they were dyeing as a means of recycling cast-off clothing and other fabrics. The results were not predictable, and the colors available were few and generally not resistant to fading. It is testimony to the importance of color to those quilters that they persevered under those conditions.

The practice of coloring fabrics with natural dyes faded as manufacturers developed chemical dyes, making colorfast fabrics in a multitude of hues easily and cheaply available. After the mid-nineteenth century, transportation was improved to the point that distribution was not a problem; cloth in all colors and patterns could even be mail-ordered. Eventually, commercial fabrics for clothing and decorating all but replaced home-dyeing. Those who continued to hand-dye their own fabrics were textile specialists interested in natural dyes or the close control of color that dyeing your own fabric allows.

The most significant advantages of the techniques described in *Dyeing to Quilt* for contemporary quilters, who have little time or space to spare, are that they are fast and efficient. Each method requires only small pieces of fabric (⅛- to ¼-yard/12 cm to 23 cm) that are dyed on a countertop or small table in bowls or cups. Compare this with the traditional immersion method, which involved large cuts of fabric in three- to five-gallon buckets, constant attendance for several hours, sometimes the addition of chemicals at certain points in the process, frequent stirrings, and other back-breaking steps. If you have experience with this type of dyeing, you will be astonished at the freedom and flexibility, with no loss of coverage, colorfastness and repeatability, offered in *Dyeing to Quilt*.

It's easy to experiment—you can try out different mixes without wasting large amounts of fabric or dye. A workstation no larger than a card table is all you need, and the largest piece of equipment is a small household bucket. You need no more than one or two yards/meters of fabric for most of the Workshops in the book. Best of all, the dyeing process is quick. It takes only a couple of minutes to mix up each dye solution, and half an hour to complete most dyeing projects. After that, the fabric can sit unattended for a few hours, or overnight if that suits your schedule, so that the dye can cure. The dye process does not have to be completed in one day, at a single sitting.

In a dyeing session, you can create up to 30 different colors, tints or shades, all with no additional chemicals, no clock-watching, no tedious stirring, and no fussing over a pot. Once you have mastered the basic techniques and learned how colors are made, you will be able to color fabrics for a complete quilt in a single day and begin sewing the next.

HOW TO USE *DYEING TO QUILT*

Dyeing to Quilt enables a quilter to create all kinds of lovely fabrics, many that are very different from commercially available alternatives. At the same time, this book helps build color confidence and encourages creative approaches to using color. Much of the guesswork is taken out of dyeing and color mixing. The results are beautiful, dependable, and repeatable.

Dyeing to Quilt offers two quick, easy dyeing methods, each of which gives spectacular results with little fuss and bother. We call them simply the bowl method and the cup method. The first creates solid colors, the second creates mottled effects. This book begins with a Quick Start to each method in Chapter 1, with easy-to-follow, step-by-step directions.

Here are six good reasons to dye your own fabrics:

- Dyeing is fast, easy, and fun.
- The colors achieved can be crisp, bright, and even, or muted and mottled, just as you please.
- Dyed fabrics are colorfast.
- Today's dyes are relatively safe, easy to use, and allow you to make *any* color.
- The colors you create are unique and not easily found in purchased fabrics.
- Dyeing is an exciting alternative to commercial fabrics.

A Ribbon Runs Through It
27" x 27" (69 cm x 69 cm)
Designed, sewn, and hand-quilted by Pat Hill, West Hills, CA
The fabrics are from several of the dyeing Workshops in Dyeing to Quilt. *The design*
makes excellent use of light and dark values. A narrow bias strip follows the curved outline
of the pieces and reinforces the feeling of movement on the surface of the quilt.

Beautiful photographs of hand-dyed fabrics show the wonderful results that are possible. Two simple Workshops introduce you to the easy mastery of each technique and the possibilities for experimentation.

Chapters 2 through 5 reveal the secrets of how colors are made. As you explore the color wheel, you learn a systematic approach to making all the colors of the rainbow. Practicing as you learn, you are enticed with ever-more sophisticated applications of your new skills—and your fabric stash grows and grows with the beautiful pieces you are dyeing. In Chapter 6 you discover how to alter the color of previously dyed fabric and how to make a patterned fabric. Finally, in Chapter 7, we present some ways just to play with color—some less structured approaches to dyeing. The book proceeds from one stage of learning to the next, so that you continuously increase your knowledge of colors and dyeing as you work through it. By the time you reach Chapter 8, Quilts to Dye For, you will have all the requisite skills to make every one of these six wonderful quilts from your own hand-dyed fabrics or to use those fabrics in your own quilt design.

Dyeing to Quilt helps you stretch your imagination and make those quilts you dream of a reality. Dyeing your own fabrics will add another dimension to your joy of creating quilts.

BASICS OF HAND DYEING— PLEASE READ BEFORE YOU BEGIN!

Part of the fun of learning a new craft is becoming familiar with the tools of the trade and the terms that accompany them.

The most exotic of the new materials you will be working with are the dyes and chemicals, some of which should be available locally. All the equipment you need for these quick methods of dyeing, such as measuring spoons and small containers, can be purchased at a supermarket, hardware store, or at flea markets. You certainly should be able to locate a suitable fabric for dyeing at your favorite quilt or sewing store. For those of you who cannot, mail order sources are listed in Appendix 6.

MATERIALS AND SUPPLIES

We have done our best to anticipate any questions you might have about any of the new products you will be using. You should refer to the information given here if any questions come up while you are shopping for materials.

Fabric

The techniques in *Dyeing to Quilt* are designed to dye small pieces of fabric, usually about ⅛ yard (12 cm) to ¼ yard (23 cm). Formulae for larger pieces of fabric are provided in Appnedix 2. Any fabric you choose for dyeing should meet the same standards you apply to all fabrics you include in a quilt. It should not be too loosely woven, or it will not take color well or hold up in a quilt. On the other hand, if it is too tightly woven, it will be difficult to quilt. It should made of a natural fiber, and should have a pleasing texture, appearance, and feel.

The best fabric for dyeing is a white 100% cotton with no permanent press finish—it prevents absorption of the dye. However, one fabric finish that is a bonus to dyeing is mercerizing, because it increases color absorption. Bleached fabric will yield slightly brighter colors than unbleached fabric.

Tip: If you live in a very dry area, add urea to your dye water to make the dye molecules bond more easily to the fabric. Dissolve 7 teaspoons of urea in a cup (8 oz) of hot water. Allow the water to cool to lukewarm before mixing. This becomes the solution to which you add dye powder. It replaces plain water.

Fabrics that are prepared for dyeing (PFD) are the best. Kona Cotton from Robert Kaufman Company bears the PFD notation on the bolt label, and is widely available in quilt and fabric shops. However, there are many other suitable, easily available, fabrics that do not have the PFD notation. The following should be easily found in quilt and fabric shops: P & B Textiles' white "Easy Care" fabric; Spring Cotton Belle, from Springs Mills; Silas Creek in white from Carolina Cotton; and Country Classics Solid in white from Beachwood. Always read the label on the end of the bolt for facts about fiber content, finishes, fabric width, and other information.

Dye suppliers also sell fabric especially for dyeing; it is sometimes listed in their catalogs as print cloth. Check Appendix 6 for mail-order sources.

Chemicals and Dyes

Soda ash or dye activator (sodium carbonate): A fixative that increases the pH of water and produces a chemical reaction that creates a permanent bond between the fibers of the fabric and the dye molecules. It is easily available from any mail order or craft store that sells dyes, as well as from swimming pool supply stores.

Synthrapol SP detergent: A strong, non-alkaline detergent used in pre-washing fabric to be dyed as well as in after-washing. When used for after-washing, it prevents loose dye particles from bonding with the fabric. It is available from dye supply sources. If Synthrapol SP is not available, you can substitute a detergent that has no alkali, bleach, brightening or degreasing agents.

Urea (organic nitrogen): A wetting agent that helps the fabric retain moisture and absorb more dye. Its use is optional except in very dry climates or in rooms with winter heat sources that may have very dry air. It is very useful for colors that take more than three hours to set.

Water softener: To be used only if you have hard water, which you can learn by calling your local water department. Metaphos water softener is available from dye suppliers. Add ¼ teaspoon to a cup (8 oz) of dye solution.

Procion MX fiber reactive dye: Procion dye is ideal for quilters because it is intended for use on natural fiber fabrics: 100% cotton, viscose rayon, silk, and linen. These synthetic dyes provide the home dyer with a wide range of clear, bright colors; the ability to be mixed with one another; the ability to cover the fabric evenly; a reasonable price; good color- and light-fastness; and ease and safety of use.

Procion dyes are easy to use, as they do not require heating on a stove; the water into which they are mixed should be between 21° to 40° Centigrade (70° to 105° Fahrenheit). In addition to the qualities listed above, these dyes are relatively non-toxic and environmentally safe. They produce intense colors and, because they can be mixed with each other, an infinite number of new colors is possible. These dyes can be stored in their original powder form for several years in a cool, dry place. Once mixed into a solution with water, they can be kept in the refrigerator for several weeks, though after four or five days they begin to lose strength. Procion dyes can be poured down the drain into a below-ground septic tank or sewer system; no special disposal procedures are necessary.

Familiar brand names for Procion dyes are PRO, Dharma, Earth Guild, and Dylon. Dye colors are generally indicated by a name and a number; the system varies depending on the manufacturer. In all cases, however, the MX number is the true indicator of the color; MX-8G is the same color whether it is named lemon yellow or sun yellow.

Many quilt shops now carry fabric dyes, as more and more of their customers explore the rewards of coloring their own fabrics for quilting. Check with your local quilt shop, and if they do not yet carry fabric dye, suggest that they should, and that they should offer classes in fabric dyeing. If your quilt shop is unable to accommodate your requests, check Appendix 6 for mail-order sources for the dye; order in 2-oz lots to begin with. (As you determine how much you will be dyeing, you may elect to buy your dye powder in larger, more economical quantities.)

Equipment

The list that follows is very comprehensive. You will see that nothing is expensive; in fact, much of what you need can be recycled from other uses. Just make sure that it is clean and watertight. Make sure, also, that you use it only for dyeing and not for food preparation. Do not use metal containers.

8 to 12 oz and 16 oz plastic drinking cups, at least 25 of each. These cups can be rinsed and reused many times. Recycled containers, such as those from yogurt or cottage cheese, can be used.

Plastic bowls, in various sizes.

Plastic measuring spoons, 1/8 teaspoon to 1 tablespoon; more than one set is helpful.

Plastic coffee scoop that holds 2 tablespoons, optional but useful.

Plastic picnic spoons for stirring and mixing.

Three plastic or glass containers that hold at least 4 cups (32 oz) of liquid.

Plastic or glass graduated measuring containers with pouring spouts, 1-cup to 4-cup (8-oz to 32-oz) capacities.

Large plastic bucket with lid, 3- to 5-gallon (12- to 15-liter) capacity.

Plastic buckets, 1- or 2-gallon (4- to 8-liter) capacity.

Plastic jug with lid, 1 gallon (4-liter) capacity.

Plastic or glass bowl, ½ gallon (2-liter) capacity.

Pitcher or other container to hold water for mixing dye solutions, of about ½ gallon (2 liter) capacity.

Plastic bags to hold dyed fabric while it cures; recycled plastic shopping bags and grocery bags are perfect. Make sure they do not have holes.

Dust mask, to meet the standards of NIOSH, National Industrial and Occupational Safety Hazards (Board). Masks should be 3M #8710 or TC-21C-132. They are available at pharmacies, hardware and paint stores, as well as from the mail order sources in Appendix 6.

Plastic drop cloth and old newspapers to cover your work surface.

Rubber gloves, elbow length: do not use thin medical gloves.

Plastic or glass containers with tight lids to store leftover dye solution in 8- to 12-oz sizes. Recycled jars, yogurt, or plastic milk containers are good choices.

Permanent felt tip marking pen, extra fine point, to label cups and fabric.

MORE CHALLENGES
26" x 26" (66 cm x 66 cm)
Designed and sewn by Joyce Mori; hand-quilted by Delores Stemple, Aurora, WV
Full-strength colors were used in this design. Bright, saturated colors combined with
black and white will always make an eye-catching quilt.

SAFETY FIRST

- Although the dyes and chemicals used in this book are relatively non-toxic, they are still industrial chemicals and should not be swallowed or inhaled. On rare occasions, dye activator or soda ash, either dry or in solution, has been known to cause mild skin irritation. Use common sense and follow our recommendations.

- Always wear a NIOSH-approved dust mask when working with dye powders and soda ash. Work in a well ventilated area, but avoid working in a breeze that might scatter dye powder. Never tear open a paper package of dye powder, and close your container of dye immediately after measuring out the amount of powder you need.

- Be especially careful handling dye powder and soda ash if you wear contacts.

- Do not smoke, eat, or drink in the area where you are dyeing to avoid accidentally ingesting any dye powder that might be airborne.

- Always wear rubber gloves when handling dye in both powder and solution forms. Both will stain the skin. If you do get dye on your hands, which we all do, several washings with Lava soap will usually remove the stains. Dye suppliers also carry hand cleanser products.

- Utensils used for dyeing should never be used for food preparation.

- Keep all chemicals and solutions out of the reach of children or pets.

- Be sure all chemicals and solutions are clearly labeled and safely stored.

- If you are pregnant or breast feeding your baby, avoid exposure to dye powders and chemicals. Have someone else measure and mix the dye powder and dye activator into solution for you.

RECORD KEEPING

So that you can quickly repeat those colors and dye effects you particularly like and avoid any you don't, make it a practice from your very first project to keep records on everything you dye. To make this easy, *Dyeing to Quilt* offers several record sheets in Appendix 1 to help you keep track of different types of projects. Make a copy of each chart, and have them duplicated onto card stock, which is heavier than plain paper. Punch holes along one long edge, and keep all your charts in a loose-leaf binder. As each project is completed, glue a small swatch of the fabrics you have dyed onto the proper chart, recording as you do so the dye name (MX number if available), the amount of water and dye powder used, the type of fabric, and anything else you wish to remember about each project. This swatch library will be your best reference for future dyeing, enabling you to repeat any color you've created.

A QUICK START

The best news about the dyeing methods in *Dyeing to Quilt* is that they are easy and quick to do. You work with small cuts of fabric in small containers. Within minutes and with a minimum of fuss, the work is done and all that is left is to wait for wonderful new colors to emerge. Anyone, even a complete beginner, can do it. There is the thrill of choosing the colors you want, and the excitement of creating something unique. Dyeing your own fabrics doubles the pleasure of making quilts: you have the one reward in coloring the fabrics, and another in placing them into your quilt.

THE VISITATION
54" x 54" (137 cm x 137 cm)
Designed, machine-pieced, and hand-quilted by Cynthia Myerberg.
Light- to medium-values of color wheel hues float in a luminous blue background, surrounded by deeper
hues that frame the quilt. The background and foreground are somewhat ambiguous, as one color bleeds
into the other. Dyeing your own fabrics makes it easy to achieve these visual contradictions.

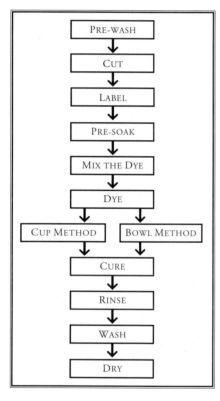

A 10-Step Quick-Dye Process

Tip: Consider soaking three or four pieces of fabric more than you need. You always have dye solution left over at the end of a dyeing session and can use it to dye this extra fabric.

In this chapter you will learn two easy dye techniques, called simply the bowl method and the cup method. The bowl method produces crisp, clear, solid colors; the cup method yields fabric with a mottled look. Each is a snap to accomplish. We titled the chapter A Quick Start, because that's exactly what it gives you. Once you understand the basic steps of the dyeing process explained here, you will be ready to dye your own colors. The two simple Workshops at the end of the chapter get you started.

THE 10-STEP QUICK-DYE PROCESS

Whether you choose the bowl method or the cup method, there are just ten quick and easy steps in the dyeing process, from preparing the fabric to setting the dye. The chart in the margin summarizes them. Read through all ten steps before you begin, then proceed at your own pace.

STEP 1—PRE-WASH THE FABRIC
Use only 100% cotton, untreated fabric for dyeing. To remove oils, dirt, and sizing left by the manufacturing process, machine wash on the hottest setting with 1 teaspoon soda ash and 1 teaspoon Synthrapol SP per 3 to 4 yards/meters of fabric. Machine dry and store the fabric until you are ready to dye.

STEP 2—CUT THE FABRIC
The projects in *Dyeing to Quilt* use "fat eighths," which are rectangles that measure 11" x 18" (28 cm x 46 cm). While working with small pieces allows you to experiment to create new colors, there will be times when you need to work with larger cuts of fabric. Use the chart in Appendix

2 to determine the correct amounts of dye solution for larger pieces of fabric.

No matter what size you decide on, you will find it convenient to cut multiples of your choice. A rotary cutter and cutting board speed up this step. Simply tearing the fabric works equally well.

STEP 3—LABEL THE FABRIC
Use a black permanent marker to number each piece of fabric to correspond with each dye solution you are going to use. The piece of fabric marked #1 will be dyed with the solution in cup #1, and so on. This will help you keep track of exactly which dye produced which color, making it easy to repeat the colors you like and to avoid the ones you don't.

STEP 4—PRE-SOAK
In a large plastic bucket (3 to 5 gallon or 12 to 15 liter), pour one gallon (3.8 liters) of hot tap water. Add 1 cup (8 oz) of soda ash and, wearing rubber gloves, stir until the soda ash has dissolved. Add the fabric pieces and soak for at least 30 minutes. (If necessary, you can leave them in the soaking solution for several days without harming the fabrics.) When you are ready to dye, wring out each piece of fabric and place it in a clean container. The pre-soak solution can be kept for several months. Simply pour it into a jug that has a lid and label it for safety.

Some of the projects in *Dyeing to Quilt* require dry fabric. For these, air-dry after pre-soaking; never use a dryer.

STEP 5—MIX THE DYE
For the projects and fabrics in *Dyeing to Quilt* we used Procion MX dyes from

PRO Chemical and Dharma. Note that final colors and strengths vary among manufacturers' brands. You may use any medium to dark color of MX dye powder you have on hand or can buy locally to proceed with the Quick Start Workshops at the end of this chapter. However, in order to duplicate some of the Workshops described in later chapters, you will need to order some specific dye powders. These are:

Red MX-8B: PRO Fuchsia 308 or
    Dharma Fuchsia Red #13
Blue MX-R: PRO Basic Blue 400 or
    Dharma Sky Blue #26
Yellow MX-8G: PRO Sun Yellow 108
    or Dharma Lemon Yellow #1
Black MX-CWA: PRO Black 608

To make up the dye solution, mix as follows:

1 teaspoon of red dye powder to 1 cup
    (8 oz) water
2 teaspoons of blue dye powder to 1
    cup (8 oz) water
3 teaspoons of yellow dye powder to 1
    cup (8 oz) water
3 teaspoons of black dye powder to 1
    cup (8 oz) water

Wearing rubber gloves and a dust mask, measure the required amount of dye powder into at least a 2-cup (16 oz) graduated measuring cup. Scoop out a teaspoon of dye powder at a time and use the handle of another spoon to level it off. Add a little lukewarm water and mix this into a paste. Fill the measuring cup to the 1-cup (8-oz) mark with more lukewarm water to make one cup of dye solution. Mix until all the dye powder is dissolved. To make

larger quantities of dye solution, simply double or triple the measures provided.

Store left-over dye solution In a secure, covered, labeled container in the refrigerator. Allow it to come to room temperature before using it. Though it is useable for several weeks, stored dye solution gets progressively weaker after the first week. Keep in mind that if you dye with a stored solution, your colors may not match up as well with the fabrics pictured in this book or with fabrics you previously dyed with fresh solution.

STEP 6—DYE THE FABRIC
Bowl Method
Use the bowl method to create solid colors, with a uniform saturation of color throughout the fabric. Place the fabric in a ½-gallon (2-liter) plastic bowl. Pour the dye solution onto the fabric. Swirl the fabric around in the dye solution several times, then squeeze out the excess dye with your hands. Put the fabric in a small plastic sandwich bag or in a grocery bag to cure.

Cup Method
Use the cup method to achieve a mottled pattern on fabric. Pour the dye solution into an 8-to 12-oz plastic or glass drinking cup, then add the fabric, pushing it into the dye solution. Leave it uncovered in the cup. Note that the size of the cup influences the degree of mottling—the smaller the cup, the more mottled the fabric will be.

STEP 7—CURE THE FABRIC
The time needed for curing—allowing the dye molecules to bond permanently with the fibers of the fabric—varies according to colors. Most are cured after just three hours. A notable exception, turquoise, or

Tip: When mixing dye powder into a solution, keep in mind that not all dye powders are alike. Some are more intense, and so have a greater tinting strength than others. Some are more difficult than others to dissolve in water. As you go through the Workshops, keep to the water-to-dye powder ratios specified. However, the more experienced you become, you may wish to modify these proportions to create desired effects.

Tip: If you need to transport your dyed fabric to a warmer place to cure, place the cups or plastic bags with the dyed fabric in a tray or box to prevent any drips or spills from staining carpets or furniture.

ART DECO
26½" x 26½" (67 cm x 67 cm)
Designed and sewn by Joyce Mori; hand-quilted by Joyce Mori and Delores Stemple, Aurora, WV
The modified fan design contains all medium value, cup-dyed fabrics in most of the colors in the
color wheel. The dark value navy acts as a neutral, setting off the design and delineating each fan.

any dye powder that contains turquoise, takes 24 hours to cure. While it cures, keep the fabric moist and make sure the room temperature is at least 65° Fahrenheit (18° Centigrade).

STEP 8—RINSE THE FABRIC

To remove as much of the excess dye as possible, remove the fabric from the bags or cups and rinse. One method of rinsing that works well is to half-fill a bucket with water in a laundry tub. Immerse the fabric, then rinse. Dump out the water and wring out the fabric. Repeat until the water is clear. You can also rinse the fabric under running water in a laundry tub or sink.

STEP 9—WASH THE FABRIC

Machine wash in hot water with 1 teaspoon of Synthrapol SP per 2 yards/meters of fabric. Run the fabric through two washing cycles. Between washes, check to see that the fabrics are not tangled. Trim any loose threads.

STEP 10—DRY THE FABRIC

Machine dry the dyed fabric. Steam-press the fabrics to rid it of any wrinkles. You will notice that once ironed, the final color is several shades lighter than it appeared when wet.

These ten steps are all you must know to dye your own fabric. Each dyeing project in *Dyeing to Quilt* follows these basic steps. Your first dyeing session may go slowly, but as you gain experience, you will learn ways to speed through the steps. For example, if you always have on hand a supply of pre-washed, pre-cut fabric, you can dye anytime the urge strikes you.

WHAT'S NEXT?

It's hard to believe that it takes so little time and space to explain the basics of our dyeing techniques, but it's true. You now have the knowledge to dye fabric with two different techniques, each with different results. In the chapters that follow, we will build on this foundation, sharing with you the results of our experiments in dyeing. We'll also introduce the basics of color theory that will help you both plan out projects and dye with confidence.

Tip: Write these formulae on an index card and put it in your laundry area.

Pre-wash—teaspoon soda ash + 1 teaspoon Synthrapol SP per 3 to 4 yards/meters of fabric

After-wash—1 teaspoon Synthrapol SP per 2 yards/meters of fabric

GAMEBOARD
20" x 20" (137 cm x 137 cm)
Designed, machine-pieced, and machine-quilted by Cynthia Myerberg.
All fabrics in this quilt were dyed using the bowl method. Three tertiary hues from the color
wheel—red-orange, blue-violet, and yellow-green—form a powerful triadic harmony when used
in appropriate proportions with one another and combined with neutral gray and black.
This small quilt is embellished with prairie points, beads, and buttons.

WORKSHOP 1.1 A QUICK START TO DYEING SOLID COLORS WITH THE BOWL METHOD

This Workshop will show you how to achieve different variations of solid color, while using the same color dye solution.

1. Pre-wash and machine-dry the fabric.
2. Label the fabric pieces #1 through #6, presoak, and wring out.
3. Pour ¼ cup (2 oz) of dye solution into the bowl. Add fabric piece #1 and swirl the fabric around in the dye solution until it is saturated, soaking up as much of the dye solution as possible with the fabric. Gently wring out the fabric letting the dye drip back into the bowl. Do not try to squeeze all the dye out of the fabric. It should be wet but not dripping. Put the fabric in a plastic bag and seal enough to keep it from drying out as it cures. Place the bag in the bucket or tray. Pour the used dye down the drain and rinse the bowl.
4. Pour ¼ cup (2 oz) dye solution into the bowl. Add fabric piece #2. Repeat the swirl and wring procedure in step 3 two times. Put the fabric in a plastic bag. Dispose of the used dye and rinse the bowl.
5. Pour ¼ cup (2 oz) dye solution into the bowl. Add fabric piece #3. Repeat the swirl and wring procedure in step 3 three

times. Put the fabric in a plastic bag. Dispose of the dye and rinse the bowl.
6. Add ½ cup (4 oz) water to the remaining dye solution. Again, pour only ¼ cup (2 oz) dye solution into the bowl. Add fabric piece #4. Swirl and wring once, as in step 3. Put the fabric in a plastic bag. Dispose of the dye and rinse the bowl. Repeat step 4 with fabric piece #5, using ¼ cup (2 oz) of dye solution. Swirl and wring twice. Repeat step 5 with fabric piece #6. Swirl and wring three times.
7. Allow the fabric to cure in the plastic bags for at least three hours. Rinse, wash, and dry each sample and press smooth with a steam iron.

RESULTS

Compare fabric pieces #1, #2, and #3. Fabric #3, which was swirled and wrung three times, is the darkest, most intense. It is also less mottled and more solid than the others. Notice how much lighter fabric pieces #4, #5, and #6 are than the first three. They were dyed in a diluted solution that reduces the intensity and value of the color. Use Record Sheet #1: Color Test Results (see Appendix 1) to keep track of your results.

Method:	Bowl method
Time:	15 to 20 minutes
Fabric:	6 pieces, each approx. ⅛ yard (12 cm)
Dye Solution:	1 cup (8 oz), in any medium-to-dark color (see p.15)
Equipment:	½-gallon (2- to 4-liter) glass or plastic bowl 6 plastic bags Bucket or tray

Tip: Before you begin a Workshop, copy the page and formulae and slip them into a plastic sleeve so that you can keep them in your work area.

Six Variations of Solid Color Using the Bowl Method

Six Variations of Mottled Color Using the Cup Method

WORKSHOP 1.2 A QUICK START TO DYEING MOTTLED COLORS WITH THE CUP METHOD

This Workshop will show you how to quickly and easily achieve six different mottled effects using the same dye solutions.

1. Pre-wash and machine-dry the fabric.
2. Label the fabric pieces #1 through #6, pre-soak, and wring out.
3. Pour ¼ cup (2 oz) of the dye solution in each of the three smaller numbered containers. Place fabric piece #1 into container #1, piece #2 into container #2, and so on. Stuff the pieces compactly down into their containers so that they are covered with dye solution.
4. Put ¼ cup (2 oz) warm water in containers #4, #5, and #6. To container #4, add 1 tablespoon of dye solution and mix. To container #5, add 1 teaspoon of dye solution and mix. To container #6, add ½ teaspoon of dye solution and mix. Put fabric piece #4 in container #4, piece #5 in container #5, and so on. Push piece #4 in its larger container up and down at least three times and turn the fabric over to help the dye solution reach the entire surface. Spread the fabric out as much as possible in the container so that the solution covers it. As with the first three cups, make sure each piece of fabric is covered as completely as possible with dye solution.
5. Allow the fabric to cure in the containers for three hours. Rinse, wash, and dry each sample and press smooth with a steam iron.

RESULTS

You will see from your samples that the more compactly the fabric is scrunched into the cup, the less evenly the dye penetrates the fabric. This means that some of the original white fabric shows through and the mottling effect is more distinct. Notice how the patterning is not as contrasting as the fabric goes lighter in color. Specific dye colors will also influence the way the mottled texture appears, as will the thickness and stiffness of the fabric and the closeness of the weave. Keep a record of which fabric was dyed in which container so that you can repeat the patternings you like best. Use Record Sheet #1: Color Test Results (see Appendix 1).

Method:	Cup method
Time:	10 minutes
Fabric:	6 pieces, each approx. ⅛ yard (12 cm)
Dye Solution:	1 cup (8 oz), any medium-to-dark color (see p. 15)
Equipment:	6 plastic cups or glass jars of varying sizes. Label the three smallest from #1 to #3 and the others as #4, #5, and #6.

Tip: Any plastic or glass container, from 4-oz glasses to yogurt cups to drinking cups to pint-size containers will do. The idea is that the fabric will be scrunched tightly in some and held loosely in others, for a broad range of mottled effects.

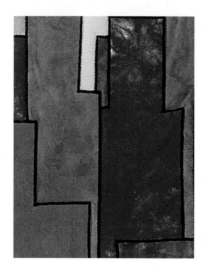

COLOR CONTROL

A key reason for dyeing your own fabric is so that you can control the colors you use in quilts. Color is, after all, one of the most important aspects of a quilt. It is possible to make a spectacular quilt with a simple one-patch design, if color is used imaginatively. Yet even the most sophisticated and original quilt concept will fail if an effective color scheme is not part of the design. This chapter provides you with the basic principles of creating color; from this you will produce a set of fabrics with which you may start creating quilts immediately.

BIG CITY SKYLINE
28" x 33" (71 cm x 84 cm)
Designed, sewn, and hand-quilted by Pat Hill, West Hills, CA
A black and white cloud-patterned fabric sets off the bright color-wheel fabrics
of the buildings. Both the cup and bowl methods were used.

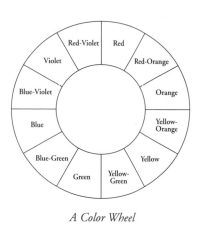

A Color Wheel

Tip: It may seem unusual to find turquoise in a list of primary colors, but it is a non-mixed dye color and can be mixed with red and yellow to produce some very bright violets and greens.

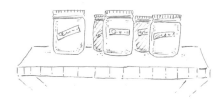

A 12-STEP COLOR WHEEL

You are about to be introduced to the basics of color—how colors are made, and how your choice of dye affects the colors you achieve. You will begin your exploration of color by dyeing the fabrics for a 12-step color wheel.

The *color wheel*, although viewed suspiciously by many quilters, is simply a selection of colors from the total color spectrum that always includes the three *primaries* of red, blue, and yellow. The primaries may be thought of as the "parents" of the color wheel, as they are the colors from which all others are mixed. A primary cannot be mixed from any other combination of colors. The colors that are mixed from the primaries, known as *secondary* and *tertiary* colors, are placed on the wheel between their "parents." Thus, the color wheel provides a basis for understanding the relationships between colors, which is integral to planning successful color schemes for your quilts. Dyeing your own color wheel will give you an invaluable foundation for understanding color mixing. (We will discuss color wheels in more detail in Chapter 4.) Turn to Workshop 2.1 at the end of the chapter to dye your first color wheel.

SELECTING DYES FOR PRIMARY COLORS

Most of the Workshops in *Dyeing to Quilt* use the three primary colors of red, yellow, and blue. These colors can be mixed in various combinations to create hundreds of other colors. The most intense primary colors are from dyes that are not mixed. (See Appendix 3 for a listing of non-mixed dyes.)

The following dyes for primary colors are non-mixed, and can be used for any of the Workshop projects in the book, particularly those in this chapter and the next. Those dyes marked with an asterisk produce the most intense, clear colors.

Yellow	*Red*	*Blue*
MX-8G*	MX-8B*	MX-R*
MX-3RA	MX-5B	MX-2G 125
MX-GR		MX-G Concentrate
MX-4G		MX-G (turquoise)

Of course, in addition to these non-mixed dyes, there are several mixed dyes that you will enjoy using to create completely new colors. Some of the Workshops that follow do just this.

ALL PRIMARIES ARE NOT THE SAME

If you carefully compare a group of reds, you will see that some of them have a violet cast. That is because they have a blue component. Other reds have an orange cast, because they lean toward yellow. Likewise, certain yellows have a green look because there is an influence of blue, or the yellow has on orange cast because it has a red component. When you study blues, some have violet overtones because of a red influence, and some look greenish because they have a yellow component.

When selecting dye powders to use as primaries, there are many to choose from. Generally, you will try to select the "purest" or "truest" hue. However, in your search for the purest hue you will soon come to realize that, like the fountain of youth, it does not exist. Actually,

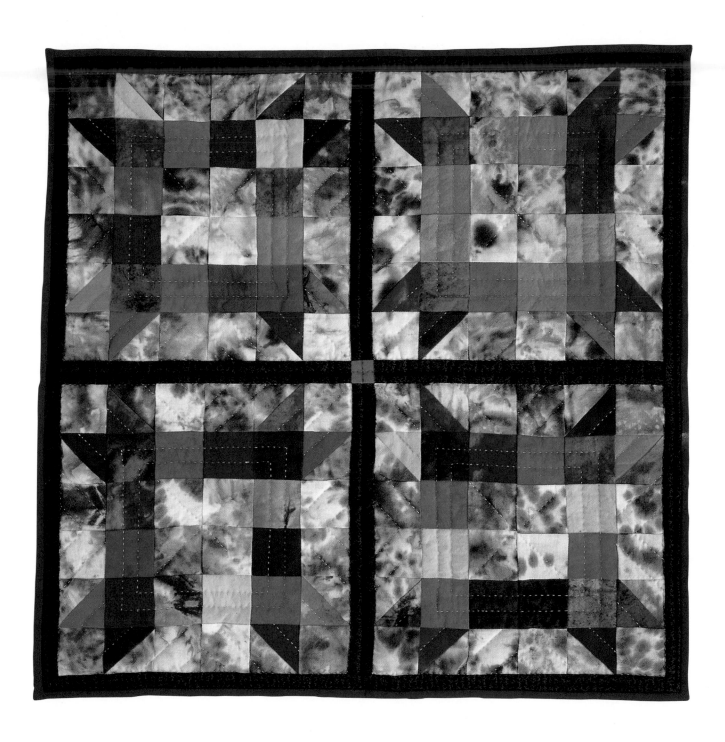

KINDERGARTEN
19" x 19" (48 cm x 48 cm)
Designed, sewn, and hand-quilted by Joyce Mori
These bright colors appear all the more intense as a result of the black and white mottled
background. Remember you wonderful crayons from kindergarten?

Round Peg in a Square Hole
28" x 28" (71 cm x 71 cm)
Designed, sewn, and hand-quilted by Pat Hill, West Hills, CA
This would be a good design for fabrics created from the Color Wheel Test Workshop in
Chapter 2. Notice the hand-quilted circle motifs that serve to reinforce the circle theme.

it is an advantage to dyers that there is no perfect color, because when you mix bluish-red with reddish-blue, you get one set of purples; but if you mix bluish-red with greenish-blue, you will get a different set of purples. Therefore, the range of colors you can create becomes almost infinite.

You can see that your choice of primary colors will determine the colors you create. A red with a yellow component combined with a yellow that has a red component will produce a bright, lively orange. If you select a red with a yellow component and a yellow with a greenish cast (blue component) the resulting color is a duller orange. The same principle follows when blue and yellow are mixed together. Some greens are in the lime green category, others are more bluish forest greens. It all depends which blue and yellow primary dye powder choices you make.

This tendency of a primary color to lean toward another color, to have a certain color component, should be the guiding principle in choosing your dye powders. This concept helps you to understand what might have gone wrong when you mixed a red and blue together but did not get the bright purple you were after.

Many dyers, in order to provide themselves more flexibility, work with as many as six different primaries that reflect the possible leanings of each color. They simply change one of the primaries to create new color wheels. As you become experienced in hand dyeing, you may want to experiment in this way.

ALTERNATIVE COLOR WHEELS AND COLOR PALETTES

Since many people think of color wheel as made up of non-mixed primary colors only, we use the term *color palette* to describe wheels made up of primary colors made from mixed dye powders.

Following are suggestions for four sets of colors. The first two are color wheels; the last two are color palettes. You made Set #1 when you dyed your first color wheel in Workshop 2.1. The additional sets show you how much freedom is possible when you dye your own fabrics; simply changing one color will give you an entirely new color wheel, as you will discover with Set #2. Sets #3 and #4 change all three of the primaries for totally different results.

SET #1 (see Figure 2.1)
Yellow (MX-8G): Dharma Lemon Yellow #1 or
    PRO Sun Yellow 108
Red (MX-8B): Dharma Fuchsia Red #13 or
    PRO Fuchsia 308
Blue (MX-R): Dharma Sky Blue #26 or
    PRO Basic Blue 400

This is the set of primaries we used for the first color wheel in this chapter. The purples and the oranges are clear. The greens are leaf greens and lime green. This basic set of primaries offers you a good range of colors all around the color wheel. But keep in mind that there is no perfect set of primaries. Some secondary and tertiary colors turn out better with one set of primaries, some with another set—there is always a trade-off. That is what makes dyeing fun, to see what you create when you try different combinations.

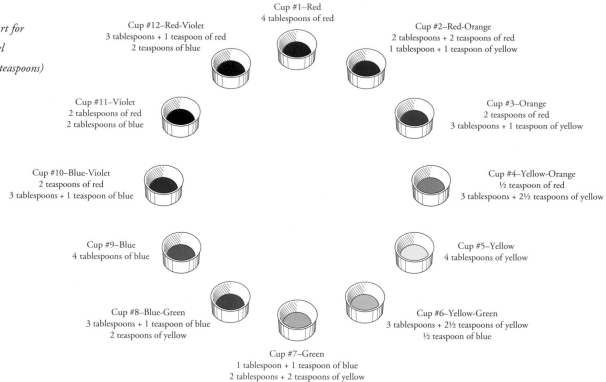

Figure 2.1

Color Mixing Chart for

Set #1 Color Wheel

(1 tablespoon = 3 teaspoons)

Cup #1–Red
4 tablespoons of red

Cup #12–Red-Violet
3 tablespoons + 1 teaspoon of red
2 teaspoons of blue

Cup #2–Red-Orange
2 tablespoons + 2 teaspoons of red
1 tablespoon + 1 teaspoon of yellow

Cup #11–Violet
2 tablespoons of red
2 tablespoons of blue

Cup #3–Orange
2 teaspoons of red
3 tablespoons + 1 teaspoon of yellow

Cup #10–Blue-Violet
2 teaspoons of red
3 tablespoons + 1 teaspoon of blue

Cup #4–Yellow-Orange
½ teaspoon of red
3 tablespoons + 2½ teaspoons of yellow

Cup #9–Blue
4 tablespoons of blue

Cup #5–Yellow
4 tablespoons of yellow

Cup #8–Blue-Green
3 tablespoons + 1 teaspoon of blue
2 teaspoons of yellow

Cup #6–Yellow-Green
3 tablespoons + 2½ teaspoons of yellow
½ teaspoon of blue

Cup #7–Green
1 tablespoon + 1 teaspoon of blue
2 tablespoons + 2 teaspoons of yellow

Use this chart to mix dye solutions for a complete 12-step color wheel. You will first need to mix basic red, blue, and yellow dye solutions. Workshop 2.1 takes you through all the steps. The proportion of dye powder to water is as follows:

Red (MX-8B): 2 cups of warm water to every two teaspoons of dye powder

Blue (MX-R): 2 cups of warm water to every four teaspoons of dye powder

Yellow (MX-8G): 2 cups of warm water to every six teaspoons of dye powder

Set #1 Color Wheel

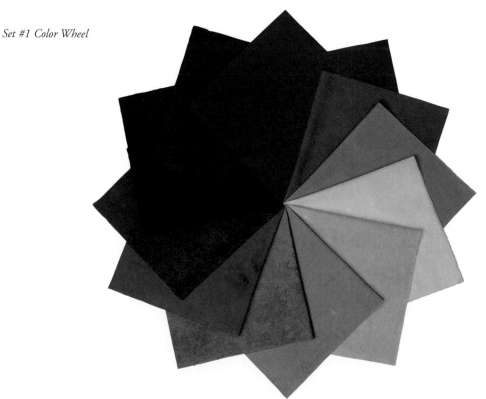

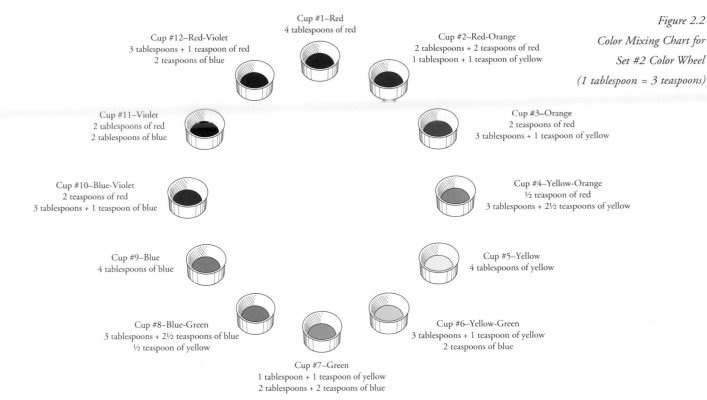

Cup #1–Red
4 tablespoons of red

Cup #12–Red-Violet
3 tablespoons + 1 teaspoon of red
2 teaspoons of blue

Cup #2–Red-Orange
2 tablespoons + 2 teaspoons of red
1 tablespoon + 1 teaspoon of yellow

Cup #11–Violet
2 tablespoons of red
2 tablespoons of blue

Cup #3–Orange
2 teaspoons of red
3 tablespoons + 1 teaspoon of yellow

Cup #10–Blue-Violet
2 teaspoons of red
3 tablespoons + 1 teaspoon of blue

Cup #4–Yellow-Orange
½ teaspoon of red
3 tablespoons + 2½ teaspoons of yellow

Cup #9–Blue
4 tablespoons of blue

Cup #5–Yellow
4 tablespoons of yellow

Cup #8–Blue-Green
3 tablespoons + 2½ teaspoons of blue
½ teaspoon of yellow

Cup #6–Yellow-Green
3 tablespoons + 1 teaspoon of yellow
2 teaspoons of blue

Cup #7–Green
1 tablespoon + 1 teaspoon of yellow
2 tablespoons + 2 teaspoons of blue

Use this chart to mix dye solutions for an alternate color wheel. You will first need to mix basic turquoise (blue), red, and yellow dye solutions. The proportion of dye powder to water for these is as follows:

Red (MX-8B): 2 cups of warm water to two teaspoons of dye powder

Blue (MX-G—turquoise): 2 cups of warm water to four teaspoons of dye powder

Yellow (MX-8G): 2 cups of warm water to six teaspoons of dye powder

Set #2 Color Wheel

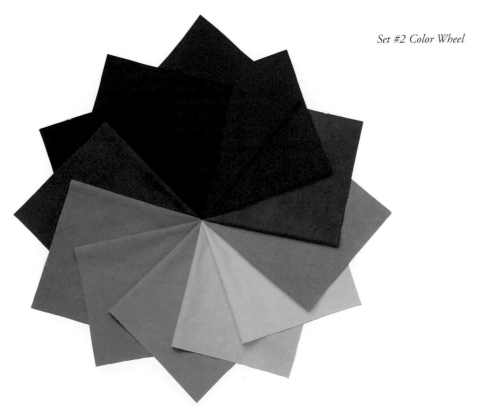

Figure 2.3
Color Mixing Chart for Set #3
Color Pallete

(1 tablespoon = 3 teaspoons)

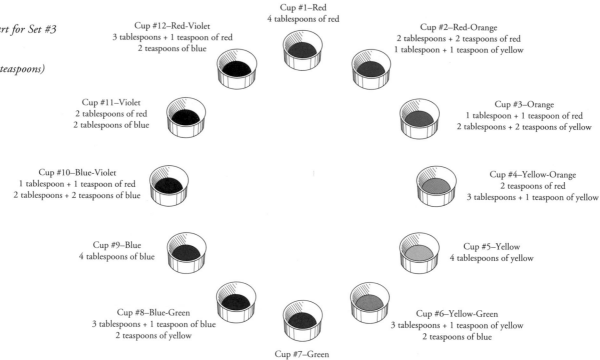

Cup #1–Red
4 tablespoons of red

Cup #12–Red-Violet
3 tablespoons + 1 teaspoon of red
2 teaspoons of blue

Cup #2–Red-Orange
2 tablespoons + 2 teaspoons of red
1 tablespoon + 1 teaspoon of yellow

Cup #11–Violet
2 tablespoons of red
2 tablespoons of blue

Cup #3–Orange
1 tablespoon + 1 teaspoon of red
2 tablespoons + 2 teaspoons of yellow

Cup #10–Blue-Violet
1 tablespoon + 1 teaspoon of red
2 tablespoons + 2 teaspoons of blue

Cup #4–Yellow-Orange
2 teaspoons of red
3 tablespoons + 1 teaspoon of yellow

Cup #9–Blue
4 tablespoons of blue

Cup #5–Yellow
4 tablespoons of yellow

Cup #8–Blue-Green
3 tablespoons + 1 teaspoon of blue
2 teaspoons of yellow

Cup #6–Yellow-Green
3 tablespoons + 1 teaspoon of yellow
2 teaspoons of blue

Cup #7–Green
1 tablespoon + 1 teaspoon of blue
2 tablespoons + 2 teaspoons of yellow

Use this chart to mix dye solutions for an alternate color palette. You will first need to mix basic red, blue, and yellow dye solutions. The proportion of dye powder to water for these is as follows:

Red (MX-GBA):	2 cups of warm water to two teaspoons of dye powder
Blue (MX-2G—Cobalt Blue 22):	2 cups of warm water to four teaspoons of dye powder
Yellow (MX-3RA—Golden Yellow 104):	2 cups of warm water to six teaspoons of dye powder

Set #3 Color Palette

Cup #1–Red
4 tablespoons of red

Cup #12–Red-Violet
3 tablespoons + 1 teaspoon of red
2 teaspoons of blue

Cup #2–Red-Orange
3 tablespoons + 2½ teaspoons of red
½ teaspoon of yellow

Cup #11–Violet
2 tablespoons + 2 teaspoons of red
1 tablespoon + 1 teaspoon of blue

Cup #3–Orange
2 tablespoons + 2 teaspoons of red
1 tablespoon + 1 teaspoon of yellow

Cup #10–Blue-Violet
2 teaspoons of red
3 tablespoons + 1 teaspoon of blue

Cup #4–Yellow-Orange
1 tablespoon + 1 teaspoon of red
2 tablespoons + 2 teaspoons of yellow

Cup #9–Blue
4 tablespoons of blue

Cup #5–Yellow
4 tablespoons of yellow

Cup #8–Blue-Green
3 tablespoons + 1 teaspoon of blue
2 teaspoons of yellow

Cup #6–Yellow-Green
3 tablespoons + 2½ teaspoons of yellow
2 teaspoons of blue

Cup #7–Green
2 tablespoons of blue
2 tablespoons of yellow

Use this chart to mix dye solutions for an alternate color palette. You will first need to mix basic red, blue, and yellow dye solutions. The proportion of dye powder to water for these is as follows:

Red (Claret):	2 cups of warm water to two teaspoons of dye powder
Blue (Navy):	2 cups of warm water to four teaspoons of dye powder
Yellow (Marigold):	2 cups of warm water to six teaspoons of dye powder

Set #4 Color Palette

SET #2 (see Figure 2.2)

Use the same yellow and red as above, but change the blue to:

Blue (MX-G turquoise) Dharma Turquoise #25 or PRO Turquoise 410

The greens are vivid and bright because the blue primary has been changed. (Remember to cure any fabrics dyed with turquoise for at least 24 hours.)

SET #3 (see Figure 2.3)

Yellow (MX-3RA): Dharma Deep Yellow #4 or PRO Golden Yellow 104

Red (MX-GBA): Dharma Chinese Red #10A

Blue (MX-2G): Dharma Cobalt Blue #22 or PRO Mixing Blue 402c

The purples are dull, because MX-GBA is a mixed dye. Some olive greens appear. The oranges are bright and vivid.

SET #4 (see Figure 2.4)

Yellow: PRO Marigold 1227

Red: PRO Claret 1197

Blue: Dharma Navy #24

All three of these dye powders are mixed colors used as primaries. They have no MX designations. The colors produced are very dull and somber; the purples are brownish, and the oranges are more gold. They might be perfect for a folk art theme. This color palette illustrates that you should be willing to try all kinds of combinations. If you change the red to fuchsia, the purples and oranges become brighter, but the color wheel stays subdued.

THE INSIDE SCOOP ON POWDERED DYE

There is a little secret in the labeling of dyes that will let you know what type of color you will get when you use the dye. Dyes with MX labeling often contain the letter G, B, or R, along with a number, as part of the notation. The letter G, when given with a blue or yellow dye, means the dye has a greenish cast. The letter B indicates a leaning toward blue, and R is for a reddish cast.

For example, cobalt blue is MX-2G, meaning that the color of the blue tends to have a greenish cast. The number 2 means the leaning is only moderate. A lemon yellow labeled MX-8G means that this yellow has a high greenish cast. If you decided to mix this blue and this yellow together, you would get a nice bright green. If you choose a different yellow, say one with a reddish cast, to mix with this blue, you might get a brownish green. Study the MX chart (see Appendix 3) and determine which dye powders to buy to achieve the results you desire.

For dyes with no MX designations, simply mix a small amount of solution, dye a piece of fabric and note the characteristics of the resulting color. Does it lean towards blue, yellow, red, green? Record the properties of the color so that you can predict how the dye will mix with another dye powder.

WHAT'S NEXT?

In this chapter, you covered the basics of color mixing. You have not only learned what a color wheel is, you have made one with your own dyed fabrics. You can tell the difference between primary, secondary, and tertiary hues. You know that there are many types of primaries, and the ones you choose will determine all the colors in their particular color wheel. Now, let us go a little further into how get our dyes to work for us—that is the key to true color control.

In order to duplicate exactly the color wheel photographed on page 28, you must use the formulas provided and the dye powders listed. You will be using the bowl method, because your goal is to achieve clear, bright colors.

1. Pre-wash and machine-dry fabric. Cut and label the pieces #1 through #12.
2. Prepare the following dye solutions in 16-oz plastic cups (see p. 15):

   6 teaspoons of yellow MX-8G per two cups (16 oz) of water

   2 teaspoons of red MX-8B per two cups (16 oz) of water

   4 teaspoons of blue MX-R per two cups (16 oz) of water

3. Use the formula chart in Figure 2.1 to make the other solutions for the color wheel from these three basic solutions (see p. 28). Each color has a name, a number and a formula. Arrange the 12 plastic cups to imitate the shape of the formula chart. Dipping from your master cups of red, blue, and yellow, measure the amounts needed for each different color into the correct cup. For example, cup #1 gets 4 tablespoons of red dye solution. Cup #2 gets 2 tablespoons plus 2 teaspoons of red dye solution and then 1 tablespoon plus 1 teaspoon of yellow dye solution. Continue until all 12 cups contain their individual mixes of dye. Stir each solution with a different plastic spoon.

4. Pour the solution from cup #1 into the plastic bowl. Add a piece of fabric to this and dye it, swirling and squeezing the fabric three times to get an intense color. Place the fabric in a plastic bag for curing, then in a clean plastic pan or pail for storage. Discard the used solution or pour it back into its cup to be disposed of later. Rinse the bowl and your gloved hands to avoid contamination of the white pieces of fabric yet to be dyed. Continue dyeing cups #2 through #4.
5. With cup #5, change to a different primary. Dye cups #5 through #8, following the directions in step 4. Rinse the bowl thoroughly before starting the third primary with cup #9. Complete the color wheel by dyeing in cups #9 through #12.
6. Allow the fabric to cure and then rinse, wash, dry and iron (see p. 15-17).

RESULTS

Arrange your fabrics in a circle to imitate the shape of the color wheel (see p. 28). Notice how bright and saturated in color each piece is. Use Record Sheet #2: 12-Step Color Wheel Results (see Appendix 1) as a guide to placing your color swatches from this project, thus completing your color wheel. Though solid colors most accurately show the exact colors mixed, you can use the cup method for this and the following Workshop.

Method:	Bowl method
Time:	1 hour
Fabric:	12 pieces, each approx. ⅛ yard (12 cm)
Dye Powders:	Yellow MX-8G, Red MX-8B, Blue MX-R.
Equipment:	3 plastic cups, each 16-oz or larger
	12 plastic cups, each 8-oz
	12 teaspoons
	Plastic bowl
	12 plastic bags
	Measuring cup
	Measuring spoons
	Rags

Tip: If you live in a dry climate, remember to add urea to the water (see p. 8).

Method: Bowl method
Time: 15 minutes
Fabric: 6 pieces each approx.
              ⅛ yard (12 cm)
Dye Solution: ½ cup of each selected
              primary color
Equipment: 6 cups
              1 bowl
              6 plastic bags

Tip: Lay a white cloth beneath your fabric when you steam press it. If any color bleeds onto the white fabric, wash the dyed fabric again. This also protects your ironing board from unwanted dye which could stain other items you iron.

If you have three primaries you want to consider for a color wheel project, the following procedure will allow you to see the mixing potential for these colors without wasting a lot of time and fabric. Before you begin, mix ½ cup (4 oz) of each primary dye solution—red, yellow, and blue.

1. Follow Steps 1-4 on page 14 to prepare the fabric for dyeing.
2. Set out the 6 cups, as in Figure 2.5.
3. Dipping from your master cups of dye solution, measure the amounts needed for each color into the correct cup. (You will notice that the secondary colors are formed by using equal amounts of two primary dye solutions).

4. Dye using the bowl method (Workshop 1.1). Cure, rinse, wash, dry, and iron the fabric, following Steps 5-10 on pages 14-17.

RESULTS

You have a sample of each primary and you can now assess its characteristics. You also have three secondary colors and you get a rough idea of whether your oranges will be bright, brownish, etc. You see if your greens will be olive, forest, or blue greens. And you note whether your purples are reddish, brownish, or bright. The examples photographed are just some of the many, many possibilities. Use Record Sheet #1: Color Test Results (see Appendix 1) to keep track of the results.

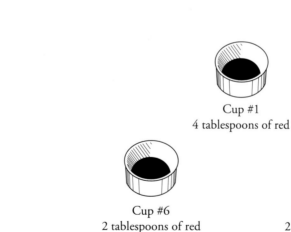

Cup #1
4 tablespoons of red

Cup #6
2 tablespoons of red
2 tablespoons of blue

Cup #2
2 tablespoons of red
2 tablespoons of yellow

Cup #5
4 tablespoons of blue

Cup #4
2 tablespoons of blue
2 tablespoons of yellow

Cup #3
4 tablespoons of yellow

Figure 2.5

Mixing Chart for a Quick Color Test

Color Wheel Test: Primary and Secondary Colors

CHAPTER 3

ANOTHER SPIN OF
THE COLOR WHEEL

In Chapter 2, you gave the color wheel a spin, practicing the concept of color mixing. You learned the basics of color mixing, and how to analyze color. In this chapter, you will learn that there is more than one purple hidden between red and blue, more than one green between blue and yellow, and more than one orange between yellow and red. You will learn how to find for yourself all the hidden variations of these secondary and tertiary hues. Your fabric stash will be like nothing you can buy in a store, just with the fabrics you'll make in these color mixing exercises.

THE POORPLE SNAKE
36½" x 36½" (93 cm x 93 cm)
Designed, machine- and hand-pieced, and hand-quilted by Cynthia Myerberg.
This scrap quilt combines many of the hues, values, and chromas we will explore in
Dyeing to Quilt. The fabrics were dyed using the cup and bowl methods. The blue-violet
snake was dyed using the cup method.

Recipes for 15 Step Color Run

Cup	Color A	Color B
#1	4T	
#2	3T + 2½tsp	½tsp
#3	3T + 2tsp	1tsp
#4	3T + 1tsp	2tsp
#5	3T	1T
#6	2T + 2tsp	1T + 1tsp
#7	2T + 1tsp	1T + 2tsp
#8	2T	2T
#9	1T + 2tsp	2T + 1tsp
#10	1T + 1tsp	2T + 2tsp
#11	1T	3T
#12	2 tsp	3T + 1tsp
#13	1tsp	3T + 2tsp
#14	½tsp	3T + 2½tsp
#15		4T

T=tablespoon

tsp=teaspoon

Tip: Plan for some uninterrupted time before you begin a color run: when working with so many cups, it is easy to lose track of where you are.

AN EXPANDED COLOR WHEEL

The standard 12-step color wheel you made in Chapter Two contained the three primary colors, with three colors between each pair of primaries. However, a more sophisticated, complex color wheel can show seven or more different gradations between two primary colors: there are seven or more oranges between red and yellow, seven or more purples between red and blue, and seven or more greens between blue and yellow.

The reason for this is that secondary colors do not have to be made of equal amounts of each of the primaries, even though you might logically assume that to be the case. As you vary the proportions of the primary colors in relation to one another, a whole spectrum of secondary and tertiary colors emerges.

The dyeing of many variations between two colors is called a *color run*. The resulting wealth of color is a boon to the quilter; you can choose the hues that you like best for your color wheel, and save the others for your fabric stash.

The photographs on pages 42-43 show nine-step color runs for each set of primaries on the first color wheel we created (p. 33). As you compare the color runs to the color wheel, you will see that the orange, purple, and green on the color wheel are not the ones in the center of the color run, in which equal amounts of both primary colors are used. There were more attractive alternatives in each case.

MIXING TWO-COLOR DYE RUNS

The mixing system you are about to learn can be used for any two colors. This wonderful set of formulae is the same for some of the remaining Workshops in the book. Once you understand it, you have the magic key to creating an unlimited palette of colors. Moreover, you can re-create any one of those colors any time you wish with complete confidence in the results, because you always use the same formulae. If you are diligent in your record-keeping, you will soon have not only a file of fabric swatches that will be the envy of any quilter, you will have an archive to which you can refer again and again.

To understand how a two-color dye run works, look at Figure 3.1. There are nine cups. Each cup contains a formula; measurements are given for Color A, which in the Workshop that follows is red, and Color B, which is blue. You will notice that the proportion of Color A to Color B gradually shifts as you move from left to right, from red to blue. The first cup is Color A only, and the last cup is Color B only. Now turn to Workshop 3.1 to make your first two-color dye run.

MAKING LONGER COLOR RUNS

Color runs do not have to be limited to nine gradations. You can increase the number of variations between the two colors to as many as 15. The shifts in color from one step to the next will be more subtle and less distinct. The formulae for a 15-Step Color Run are in the margin.

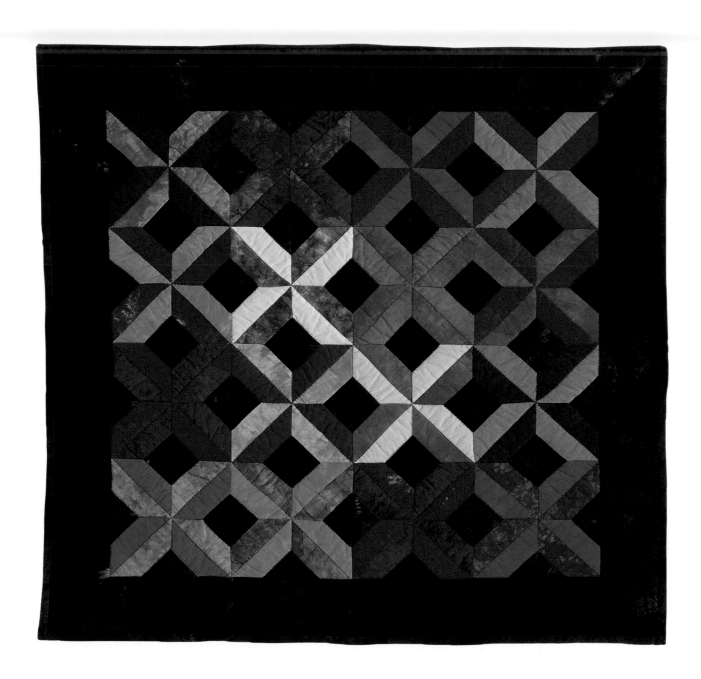

BEYOND THE RAINBOW
40" x 40" (102 cm x 102 cm)
Designed and machine-pieced by Cynthia Myerberg; hand-quilted by Delores Stemple, Aurora, WV
Workshop 3.1, done with both the cup and bowl methods, provided all the pure hues for this quilt.
The use of black with these undiluted hues sets up a strong contrast.

MIXING BETWEEN ANY TWO COLORS

Now that you know how to do a two-color dye run, the entire world of color is open to you. You can take all the information you have just learned and begin to create some colors of your own. You will enjoy making up your own combinations. Here are some suggestions for two-color combinations to get you started.

Yellow MX-4G and Scarlet MX-BRA
Yellow MX-8G and Scarlet MX-BRA
Blue MX-G and Scarlet MX-BRA
Red MX-GBA and Navy
PRO Hollandaise 1203 and Turquoise MX-G
Green MX-CBA and Violet

WHAT'S NEXT?

By the time you have completed the Workshop and tried out other color runs, you will be at ease with the process of dyeing. You will have repeated it until you are perfectly comfortable with the bowl method. And, you have a good foundation in color theory. You know how different colors are made, and you have begun to explore the many possibilities that await you as you mix your own hues. However, you've worked with only two colors thus far; in the next chapter, you will learn how to control the value of a color, how to make it darker or lighter, as well as how to vary the intensity, or brightness.

Cup #1
4 tablespoons of Color A

Cup #2
3 tablespoons + 2½ teaspoons of Color A
½ teaspoon of Color B

Cup #3
3 tablespoons + 1 teaspoon of Color A
2 teaspoons of Color B

Cup #4
2 tablespoons + 2 teaspoons of Color A
1 tablespoon + 1 teaspoon of Color B

Cup #5
2 tablespoons of Color A
2 tablespoons of Color B

Cup #6
1 tablespoon + 1 teaspoon of Color A
2 tablespoons +2 teaspoons of Color B

Cup #7
2 teaspoons of Color A
3 tablespoons + 1 teaspoon of Color B

Cup #8
½ teaspoon of Color A
3 tablespoons + 2½ teaspoons of Color B

Cup #9
4 tablespoons of Color B

Figure 3.1

Mixing Chart for a Two-Color Dye Run Using Primaries

WORKSHOP 3.1 A TWO-COLOR DYE RUN USING PRIMARIES

This Workshop will show you how to dye seven gradations between two primary colors. You will be delighted with the subtle differences that occur as a color moves from one primary toward the next. When you finish the dye runs between all three primaries, you will have completed 27 steps; the run consists of seven gradations between the two primaries, for a total of nine colors in each run. Though you can use the cup method, the differences between the resulting colors may be more difficult to see.

1. Follow Steps 1-4 on page 14 to prepare the fabric for dyeing. Number the pieces of dry fabric from #1 through #9 prior to soaking.

2. Follow the formulas below to mix the dyes for the primary colors in 32-oz containers (see also p. 15)

   Red (MX-8B)

   1 tablespoon + 1 teaspoon red

   4 cups (32 oz) warm water

   Blue (MX-R)

   2 tablespoons + 2 teaspoons blue

   4 cups (32 oz) warm water

   Yellow (MX-8G)

   4 tablespoons yellow

   4 cups (32 oz) warm water

   This is enough dye solution for all 27 steps of the color runs, though you do only 9 steps at a time.

3. Stir the red dye solution and pour 1½ cups (12 oz) into one of the 16-oz plastic cups. Do the same with the blue dye solution. Set the blue dye off to the side.

4. Set up your cups in rows as shown in Figure 3-1. Measure dye into each cup as indicated by the formulae shown:

cup #1 gets 4 tablespoons of red dye solution and no blue dye solution; cup #2 gets 3 tablespoons plus 2½ teaspoons of red dye solution and ½ teaspoon of blue dye solution, etc. Fill cups #1 through #8 with the required amount of red dye solution

5. Fill cups #2 through #9 with the required amount of blue dye solution, referring to the chart.

6. Stir the dye solutions in each cup, using a different spoon for each. Pour the dye from cup #1 into the bowl. Put the fabric #1 in the bowl and dye it using the bowl method (page 15). Swirl the and squeeze the fabric three times. Pour the used dye solution back into its cup to be disposed of at the end of the dyeing session, or discard the solution immediately.

7. Rinse out the bowl. (If you are not near a water source, you can wipe the bottom and sides of the bowl thoroughly with a rag.)

8. Dye fabric pieces #2 through #9, following steps 5 and 6.

9. Allow the fabrics to cure for at least 3 hours. Rinse, wash, dry and iron.

RESULTS

Place your fabric samples on a tabletop in order, #1 through #9. Study them carefully to select the best violet, red-violet, and blue-violet for a color wheel; compare your choices with ours. You might decide on different selections—there is no right or wrong choice. As you have time, perform the color runs between red and yellow and yellow and blue.

Method: Bowl method, though dye colors are mixed in cups

Time: 30 to 40 minutes

Fabric: 9 pieces, each approx. ⅛ yard (12 cm)

Dye Solution: See step 2

Equipment: 3 large containers (32 oz)
            2 plastic cups, each 16-oz
            9 plastic cups
            9 plastic spoons
            9 plastic bags
            Measuring spoons
            ½ gallon (2 liter) glass or plastic bowl

Tip: Work with one dye color at a time. Measure the red dye into all the cups that require it. Then go through the procedure with the blue dye. Remember to wash the measuring spoons before you proceed to the second color, in this case blue. Also, some dyers find it easiest to measure all the tablespoons first, then the teaspoons and finally the half-teaspoons.

RECORD KEEPING

As you select the three best colors in each run for a color wheel, be certain to match the number of each fabric swatch to its formula number. Record the formula on Record Sheet #2: 12-Step Color Wheel Results in Appendix 1, onto which you have affixed swatches of each color.

As you finish all three of the dye runs using the primaries, fill in Record Sheet #3: 27-Step Color Run Results, mounting swatches of each fabric in the large rectangles according to the formula for each on the two lines beneath.

Variations

The color runs pictured thus far in the chapter were done with the suggested primary dye powders for Set #1 in Chapter 2 (page 28). Try doing some color runs with primary dye powders in the other sets. If you compare the color run from Set #1 between blue and yellow with the color run between blue and yellow using the primaries of Set #2, you will be able to see how the selection of a dye powder affects the resulting mixed color. Remember to complete record sheets for every color run you execute.

Two-Color Dye Runs for Each Primary—Red to Blue, Blue to Yellow, Yellow to Red

CHAPTER 4

MODIFYING COLORS

The colors you have worked with in the Workshops up to this point have been the primaries—red, blue, and yellow. The only alteration you have made to the dyes is to mix two of them together in varying proportions to make new colors. There is much more to the study of color than that. In this chapter, we help you understand more about color by analyzing its properties. Once you know how a color is made up, it becomes easy to duplicate using dyes.

LOU'S VINE
26" x 29" (66 cm x 74 cm)
Designed, sewn, and hand-quilted by Joyce Mori
A color run, using the cup method, between purple and yellow (complements) creates the
fabric for this strip-pieced background. Notice the dull, browned versions of these mixed colors.
A pure bright purple was used for the border to frame the design.

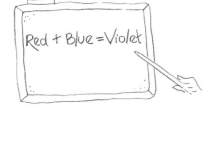

THE LANGUAGE OF COLOR

The word *color*, for artistic purposes, is imprecise. In order to better describe the nature of specific colors, special terms—hue, value, and chroma—are necessary. *Hue* is simply the name of a color, such as red or orange. It is interchangeable with the word color.

As we have seen, the *primary* hues are red, blue, and yellow. When you mix two primaries, a *secondary* hue is produced: red and yellow make orange, blue and yellow make green, red and blue make violet.

When a primary hue is mixed with a secondary hue, a *tertiary* hue results: red and violet make red-violet; blue and violet make blue-violet; red and orange make red-orange; yellow and orange make yellow-orange; blue and green make blue-green; yellow and green make yellow-green. Primary, secondary, and tertiary hues can be mixed with each other to produce an infinite number of new hues.

Some dyers feel that the secondary and tertiary colors produced by mixing dyes together are not as bright as if these colors were created from a purchased dye powder. That can be true, but, on the other hand, the purchased secondary and tertiary colors can sometimes appear too bright. Although you may eventually decide to purchase a wider range of dye powders, the concepts of mixing dyes presented in this book allow you to create an infinite range of beautiful colors without having to purchase so much dye, and mixing your own colors leads you to a better understanding of the relationships between colors.

RELATIONSHIPS BETWEEN COLORS

Color wheels help us understand the relationship between colors. The primary colors—red, yellow, and blue—are located an equal distance from one another around the wheel. Centered between two primary hues is a secondary hue, and between a primary hue and a secondary hue is a tertiary hue.

HUE

Hues are either warm or cool. Warm hues are the fire colors—yellow, orange, and red. Cool hues are reminiscent of water, grass, or the sky. In your quilts, warm hues advance (strike your eye first), while cool hues recede. Sometimes the warmth or coolness of a hue is affected by the hues that surround it. Violet, a cool hue, will seem warm when placed next to a cool gray.

VALUE

Value refers to the lightness or darkness of a color *when compared to a continuous white to black scale.* Pink is a light value of red, burgundy a dark value. The value of a hue can change, however, based on the hues and values that surround it. The lightest value used in one quilt might be the darkest value found in another quilt. To achieve lighter values you add more water to a dye solution or use less dye powder when making the solution. If you desire a darker value than a dye solution can produce, you must add black to that solution. Light values are called *tints* or pastels, dark values are called *shades.* You would probably not be pleased if the fabrics in a quilt were all of dark values; you would want to add some light or medium value fabrics to provide interest to the design. It is possible, simply by varying and controlling the values of different colors, to emphasize a design, to achieve depth, luminosity, contrast, and movement.

CHROMA

Chroma, or *intensity*, refers to the brightness of a hue. The primary hues are usually the most intense. The chroma of a hue can be reduced by adding black, brown, gray or the hue's complement to it; the reduced chromas of a hue are known as *shades* and *tones*. Consider the use of chroma in the quilt on page 86. Look at the dominant color of the two zigzags to the right and left of the quilt. We might call the color of this fabric burgundy, claret, mulberry, or wine. Technically, however, it can be described as follows: a shade of the hue red; a red with a bluish cast, which has had its chroma reduced by the addition of black to the red dye powder to create this hue of darker value (a shade). Whew!

Of course, we do not usually use descriptions like this. So why would dyers and quilters need to know terms that describe the characteristics of a color? Because in order to duplicate a color well, we need to be able to see and analyze the properties of that color. To recreate the burgundy in the quilt on page 86, an analysis tells us that we need to start with a red dye powder that has a bluish cast. The dye solution must be used at full strength because we want a dark value. Since the color we want is not bright, we need to add black, gray, or the color's complement to it.

MORE RELATIONSHIPS BETWEEN COLORS

Analogous colors (hues) are any three to five colors next to one another on the color wheel that share a common hue. Blue, blue-green, and green are analogous hues; they are next to one another on your color wheel, and they all contain blue. Analogous colors add harmony and tranquillity to a quilt; you can't go wrong with such a color scheme. Also, transparent effects, those in which colors seem to overlap one another, can be created by the clever use of analogous hues.

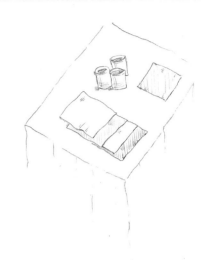

Hues that are opposite each other on the color wheel are called *complements*. Examples of complements are red and green, yellow and purple, red-orange and blue-green, and so on. Complementary hues, when used together provide the greatest contrast possible in the color wheel. They set up visual tension; use them for dynamic effects. In quilt design, it is best not to use them in equal amounts; choose one of the complements to be the most dominant. Look at the quilt on page 45 to see how well complements are used.

As you begin designing hand-dyed quilts, you will want to be able to fine-tune the hues of your fabrics. The Workshops at the end of this chapter will acquaint you with the way these properties of color can be altered in the fabrics you dye. To begin, follow Workshop 4.1 to mix a single color in three different values.

A MORE COMPLETE SET OF VALUES OF A SINGLE COLOR

Once you have a set of value gradations—full, medium, and light—of a color, it is easy to expand this into as many as eight different values of that same color. These eight values are what we call "even steps;" they progress very subtly from the lightest to the darkest—there is no sudden shift from one value to another.

Recipes for Mixing Complementary
Colors for a Color Run

Color	*Complement*
Red:	Green:
1½ cups	1 cup yellow
	½ cup blue
Yellow:	Violet:
1½ cups	1 cup red
	¾ cup blue
Blue:	Orange:
1½ cups	¼ cup red
	1¼ cups yellow
Red-violet:	Yellow-green:
1¼ cup red	1¼ cup + 3 table-
¼ cup blue	spoons yellow
	1 tablespoon blue
Blue-violet:	Yellow-orange:
1¼ cups blue	1¼ cups + 3 table-
¼ cup red	spoons yellow
	1 tablespoon red
Blue-green:	Red-orange:
1¼ cups blue	1 cup yellow
¼ cup yellow	½ cup red

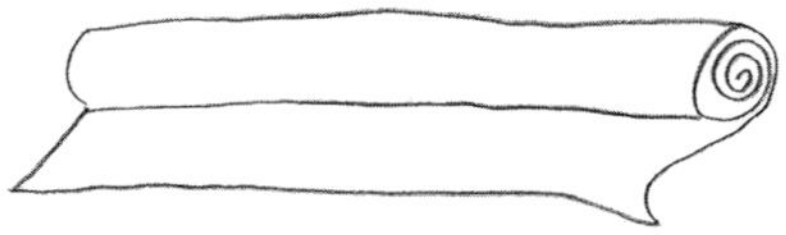

To obtain even steps, the trick is to dilute the dye solution in standard increments through the entire eight steps. Workshop 4.2 explains how.

MIXING COLORS TO CHANGE CHROMA (INTENSITY)

Do you resist using orange or yellow in your quilts because of their inherent brightness? You may find these colors more palatable when you change their chroma or intensity. Chroma refers to the brightness or dullness of a color. The different gradations of chroma are known as the tones of a hue.

There are several ways to reduce the intensity of a color. The addition of black, brown or gray to a color to make it duller, as you will see in Workshop 4.3, is the simplest.

CHANGING CHROMA BY MIXING A COLOR WITH ITS COMPLEMENT

You can also tone down a hue's chroma by adding a small amount of its complementary color. For example, when blue, the complement of orange, is added to orange, the orange becomes terra cotta, rust, or pumpkin. The more of a color's complement you add to it, the more you dull or neutralize it.

In the progressions opposite, the two pure colors on each end become gradually duller and more neutral as they move toward the center. As the chroma changes, new colors emerge. To create these color runs, use the magic formula you learned in Chapter 3 for a two-color run with nine steps. (See Figure 3-1.)

Look at the color wheel on page 28 to review complementary pairs.

red/green	red-orange/blue-green
violet/yellow	yellow-orange/blue-violet
blue/orange	yellow-green/red-violet

Once you have decided which set of complementary colors you wish to use, make up enough of your solutions to complete the project. The recipes are shown in the margin. Designate one of the dyes Color A and the other Color B, then follow the formulae for mixing the solutions for each step (see Figure 3.1). Record the formulae and enter color swatches on Record Sheet #3 in Appendix 1.

WHAT'S NEXT?

If you have followed along with the projects in these first four chapters, you should have a good understanding of color mixing, color theory, and how one color relates to another. Once you begin to analyze a color with an educated eye, you will never look at color in the same way again. When you see an appealing hue, you will know what color wheel hue or color family it is closest to, whether it is a tint, shade or tone of that hue, or if its chroma has been changed by the addition of black, brown, gray, or a complement. You will find this knowledge extremely valuable when planning color schemes. In the next chapter, we will talk about neutrals and their importance in overall quilt design.

Primaries and Complements: Blue to Orange, Red to Green, Yellow to Violet

HARLEQUIN SKY
23" x 23" (58 cm x 58 cm)
Designed, machine-pieced and machine-quilted by Cynthia Myerberg.
Value and chroma were altered in the colors that make up this quilt, giving it a
Southwestern feel. The terra cotta is a light value of red-orange, with a few drops of turquoise added.
A small amount of violet was added to the yellow to dull it to gold.

WORKSHOP 4.1 MIXING THE SAME COLOR IN THREE VALUES

This Workshop will show you how to mix three values (light, medium, and dark) of the same color.

1. Follow Steps 1-4 on page 14 to prepare the fabric for dyeing.
2. Measure dye solution into the 3 cups as follows:

   Cup #1: ¼ cup (2 oz) of dye solution (full value)

   Cup #2: 1 tablespoon of dye solution plus 3 tablespoons of water (medium value)

   Cup #3: ½ teaspoon dye solution plus ¼ cup (2 oz) water (light value)

   Pour the leftover dye back into the storage container.
3. Pour the dye from cup #1 into the bowl. Dye the fabric with the bowl technique by swirling and squeezing it three times.
4. Place the fabric in a plastic bag to cure. Throw away the dye and rinse the bowl.
5. Repeat the process for the other two pieces of fabric using the dye solution from the appropriate numbered cup.
6. Cure, rinse, wash, dry and iron your dyed fabric samples.

RESULTS

Lay your three finished samples out side by side. Examine the differences between the full, medium, and light values of one hue. You will see that the medium and light values of a hue will be more appropriate for some of your quilt designs than would the full value.

Method	Bowl method
Time:	15 minutes
Fabric:	3 pieces, each approx. ⅛ yard (12 cm)
Dye Solution:	½ cup (4 oz), in any medium-to-dark color
Equipment:	3 plastic cups, labeled #1 through #3
	Plastic or glass bowl

Three Values of Same Color

WORKSHOP 4.2 MIXING EIGHT VALUES OF THE SAME COLOR

Method: Cup or bowl method

Time: 30 minutes

Fabric: 8 pieces, each approx.
             ⅛ yard (12 cm), labeled
             #1 through #8

Dye Solution: ½ cup (4 oz) dye solution

Equipment: 8 plastic cups
             2-cup (16 oz) container
             1-cup (8 oz) measure
             ¼-cup (2 oz) measure
             Measuring spoons
             Plastic bags (bowl
             method only)

Tip: Note that if you use a mixed color, you will need double the amount given with the formula on the chart for the Nine-Step Color Run on pages 40-41. As an example, let's say you choose the blue-violet #6. The formula for color #6 is 1 tablespoon + 1 teaspoon red dye solution and 2 tablespoons + 2 teaspoons of the blue dye solution. To do 8 gradations, you will need 2 tablespoons +2 teaspoons of red dye solution and 4 tablespoons + 4 teaspoons of the blue dye solution; this will equal 1/2 cup (4 oz) of dye solution. See also Appendix 4.

For this Workshop, you can use any dye you like. You may like to choose one of the stock solutions from Chapter One (Step 5, page 15), or one of the mixed solutions of the Nine-Step Color Run from Chapter Three. You need ½ cup (4 oz) of any dye solution.

1. Follow Steps 1-4 on page 14 to prepare the fabric for dyeing.
2. Line up the plastic cups in a row and number them #1 through #8.
3. Pour the ½ cup (4 oz) of dye solution into the 1-cup (8 oz) measure, then pour ¼ cup (2 oz) of this solution into cup #1.
4. Pour ¼ cup (2 oz) of warm water into the original cup of dye solution and mix. You now have ½ cup (4 oz) of solution again; although this solution is not as strong as the original. Pour ¼cup (2 oz) of this solution into cup #2.
5. Pour ¼ cup (2 oz) of warm water into the original cup of dye solution and mix. You now have ½ cup (4 oz) of solution again, but the solution keeps getting weaker with each step. Pour ¼ cup (2 oz) of this solution into cup #3.
6. Repeat this process of using ¼ cup (2 oz) of dye solution and replacing that with ¼ cup (2 oz) of warm water until all eight cups contain solution. Discard what is left after the last cup has been filled.
7. Dye the fabric with either the bowl or cup method. Be sure you dye fabric #1 with the solution from cup #1, so that

you can keep track of which solution produced which effect.

8. Allow the fabric to cure and then rinse, wash, dry, and iron (see pages 15-17).

RESULTS

Spread out your dyed fabric swatches and arrange them in order from the lightest to the darkest. Although the gradations are subtle from one color to the next, there is a tremendous difference between the first and last samples. The light values look very unlike the swatches dyed at full strength. Use Record Sheet #4: 7- to 15 - Step Color Run Results (see Appendix 1) to record the results.

VARIATIONS

1. You can combine the bowl and the cup method in this Workshop. We suggest doing the odd numbered cups with one method and the even numbered cups with the other method.
2. You may do fewer than eight values of a color. You could do the first four values, or you might do only the odd- or even-numbered values. Even if you are not going to do all eight value gradations, we suggest that you line up all eight cups and fill them as instructed, then dye fabric for only the steps you wish. Afterwards, you might want to mix the unused dye solutions together and dye a fat quarter of fabric, using whichever method, the cup or bowl, that you prefer.

Eight Values of Same Color

Gray Matters
36½" x 36½" (93 cm x 93 cm)
Designed and machine-pieced by Cynthia Myerberg; hand-quilted by Delores Stemple, Aurora, WV.
Neutral tones created from color runs between the complementary hues of red and green and between yellow
and violet provide the rich background colors for this contemporary design. The tertiary colors of blue-green,
yellow-green, and red-violet are intensified when juxtaposed with the neutralized hues.

This Workshop will show how adding black makes a hue not only darker, but duller. To experiment further, repeat using Brown MX-CRA instead of black. To make gray, add ¼ cup (2 oz) of black dye solution to ¾ cup (6 oz) water.

1. Work with one set of cups at a time. Measure dye solution and stir:

   Cup #1: ¼ cup (2 oz) red

   ½ teaspoon black

   Cup #2: ¼ cup (2 oz) red

   2 teaspoons black

   Cup #3: 3 tablespoons red

   1 tablespoon black

2. Place fabric #1 into cup #1. Push the fabric down until it is submerged in solution. Repeat with fabrics #2 and #3.

3. Following the formulae above, substitute blue dye for the red and measure the cor-rect amounts of blue and black dye into the second set of cups. Dye three fabric swatches as in step 2.

4. Substituting yellow for red, measure the correct amounts of yellow and black dyes into the final set of cups. Dye the remaining set of fabric.

5. Allow all three sets of fabric to cure, then rinse, wash, dry and iron them.

RESULTS

The addition of even a tiny bit of black darkens the color noticeably. By the final sample, the color has changed so much from the original as to appear to be a different hue entirely. However, it will blend beautifully with other tints and shades of the color. Use Record Sheet #4 (see Appendix 1) to record the formulae and results.

Method:	Cup method
Time:	30 minutes
Fabric:	9 pieces, each approx. ⅛ yard (12 cm), three labeled as #1, three as #2, and three as #3
Dye Solution:	¾ cup (6 oz) red, ¾ cup (6 oz) blue, ¾ cup (6 oz) yellow, and ½ cup (4 oz) black
Equipment:	Nine plastic cups, three labeled as #1, three as #2, and three as #3

To create the fabrics photographed, double the dye solution amounts in cup #3 using any primary color plus black. Do eight even-step gradations to make tones (see Workshop 4.2).

Eight-Color Gradation by Adding Black

NEUTRALS

No matter how much you love color, you can't make a successful quilt from brilliant hues alone; it would be too garish. Neutrals are those colors used to balance and soften a color scheme; they make strong, saturated colors stand out rather than fight with one another. Though creating neutrals is not what immediately comes to mind when we think of hand dyeing our own fabrics, the wonderful effects possible add a richness that is difficult to find in commercial fabrics.

FALL COMES TO MICHIGAN
33" x 37" (84 cm x 94 cm)
Designed and sewn by Joyce Mori; hand-quilted by Delores Stemple, Aurora, WV
The North Wind block is made in brown, rust, and blue fabrics.
Some of the browns were dyed using Workshop 5.1.

WHAT ARE NEUTRAL COLORS?

The technical definition of a neutral is a color without hue. Gray, black, and white are familiar neutrals. Many quilters include browns, beiges, taupes, and unbleached muslin as well. Very little appears in quilting books about neutral colors and how to use them in your quilts. Most quilters are unaware of the range of colors that can be utilized as neutrals because such colors simply are not available commercially.

One of the wonderful aspects of dyeing your own fabric is that you have the capacity to create neutrals containing subtle nuances of other colors. Instead of a bland gray, for example, you can dye blue-grays, reddish-grays, yellow-grays, whatever suits your color scheme best. If you are working with a palette of reds and blues, the transitional neutral between the two colors could be a gray with either a strong bluish or reddish cast. Customized neutral colors can set your quilt apart. In some cases, they are the answer to making a color scheme work.

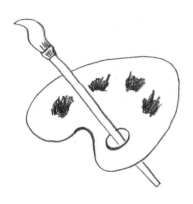

UNIQUE NEUTRALS ARE WITHIN YOUR REACH

How can you achieve these spectacular neutral colors? There are many ways, most of which you will be familiar with by now, having worked through so many Workshops.

The easiest way is the most obvious—you can buy dye powders in neutral colors such as black, brown, and beige. Study a piece of fabric you have dyed with a specific neutral color dye powder to see if it has a cast of another color. Many black dye powders have either greenish or purplish casts; if you wanted to emphasize that leaning, you would add more of the respective color to the dye. If, on the other hand, you wanted a darker, duller black, you could add the complement of the green or purple.

You can also modify any color you mix to make it more neutral. Some artists term any color with added black a neutralized color. The more black you add to a color, the more you reduce its intensity and make it neutral. The color becomes darker.

Some of the Workshops in earlier chapters will produce some very interesting neutrals. For example, it is possible that you could make some very dull brownish-violets in your color runs, depending on the particular red and blue you mixed. These violets can be diluted or neutralized even more by adding black (a neutralizing color) or yellow (the complement of violet). The range is extended so that the brownish-violets become similar to purple-blacks or grays.

Warm and lively browns can be made from mixing all three primary colors together. At the end of a dyeing session, simply pour all your primary-color dyes into one cup, then dye some fabric in the resulting blend. If you then go on to perform a three or eight color value run with this left-over dye, you will make even more neutrals. At each step in the run, the colors will tend to change; this is especially noticeable if you use the cup method. You will achieve some totally unexpected but wonderful results. The dye solution seems almost to separate into individual

NEUTRAL GROUND
33½" x 33½" (85 cm x 85 cm)
Designed and machine-pieced by Cynthia Myerberg; hand-quilted by Delores Stemple, Aurora, WV
The neutral brown in this quilt came from a color run between yellow (MX-8G) and violet (red MS-BRA and blue MX-R). Six to eight values of neutral brown, blue-green, and terra cotta create the colorwash effect. One block, with different orientations, is used to make this quilt, but the shift in hue and value give it an ambiguous surface design.

colors, resulting in a mottled fabric with hints of several colors in it. Most times the colors you get with this process are one of a kind.

Brown dyes are easily adapted to your special needs. You can make a brown more rusty-colored by adding red. Conversely, you can take a reddish-brown and dull it by adding green. What you do depends on the result you wish to achieve.

Finally, you can purchase neutral fabrics and use them as is or overdye them. As you read the section on overdyeing in Chapter 6, you will find some more ideas for neutralizing colors. You will find suggestions that are especially applicable to fabrics whose colors are not pleasing to you.

Solid neutral fabrics are a good place to show off a quilting design. Quilting often does not show up well on printed fabrics or on the mottled fabrics, so if you want to call attention to your quilting, put it on a neutral background.

MIXING COMPLEMENTARY COLORS TO CREATE NEUTRALS

The neutral or neutralized hues are those colors in the center part of the color run between complementary colors (see page 49). The two colors on either end of the run remain unaffected. Next to these pure hues, you begin to get the dulled, browned or earth-tone versions of the

colors. If you want only the browns or neutrals, then just do a set of the center three or four colors in the cups. However, make some medium and light values of these hues to provide a variety of useful fabric colors. The cup method will give you a multicolor mix. The bowl method will blend the colors more smoothly for a grayer look. Either method works well. Try both to see what suits your taste.

We have only been able to show you a small sample of the color combinations and color runs in this book. The more you experiment with other color combinations, the more spectacular your neutral colors will be. If you have not done any of the color runs between complementary pairs, now would be a good time to try them. You will find yourself using neutral fabrics often in your quilts, once you see the wonderful variety of neutrals that you can create.

WHAT'S NEXT?

Now that you've added an understanding of neutrals to your general knowledge of color theory, you are ready to begin making quilts. However, because our techniques are so simple, and because we know you will be yearning for more techniques, having mastered the ones we've shown you so far, we are going to explain some fairly exotic methods for overdyeing fabrics and creating textures. After that, we tell you how to throw out all the rules and just play with color—have fun with it.

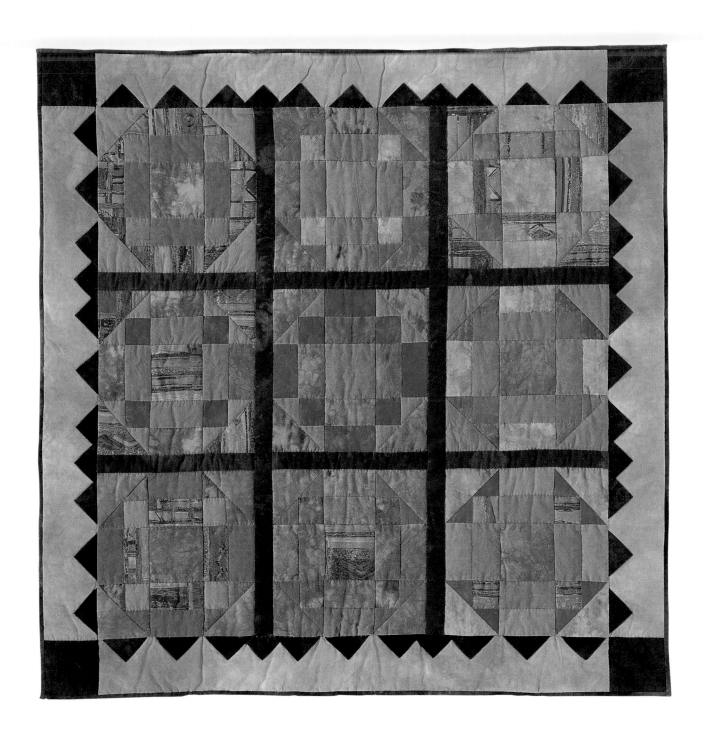

Thanks to Canada
33" x 33" (84 cm x 84 cm)
Designed and sewn by Joyce Mori; hand-quilted by Delores Stemple, Aurora, WV
This yellow-orange commercial fabric, purchased in Canada, combines beautifully with
the blue and orange fabrics created with a color run between these two complements.
All the colors in the quilt are dulled as a result of this dyeing process.

WORKSHOP 5.1 MIXING PRIMARIES TO MAKE NEUTRALS

●●●

Method: Cup method

Time: 30 minutes

Fabric: 11 pieces, each approx.
         ⅛ yard (12 cm)

Dye Powders: 1 teaspoon each of blue
         and yellow
         1½ teaspoons of red

Equipment:. 11 plastic cups
         11 plastic spoons
         Measuring spoons

This Workshop is designed to create lovely rusts, mellow browns, and gold. Three dye solutions are mixed in a single cup; Figure 5.1 details the quantities of each dye solution for each cup.

Red (MX-BRA)   Dharma Scarlet #9 or PRO Scarlet 300

Yellow (MX8G)   Dharma Lemon Yellow #1 or PRO Sun Yellow 108

Blue (MXR)   Dharma Sky Blue #26 or PRO Basic Blue 400

These solutions are made with a different proportion of dye powder to water than usual. You may change your amounts of dye powder per cup of water depending on the intensity of the dye powder and the final effect you want to achieve. This is something you will want to experiment with on your own as you do more and more dyeing. However, for this project, use one teaspoon of dye powder to one cup (8 oz) of water for the blue and yellow, and 1½ teaspoons of dye powder to one cup (8 oz) for the red.

1. Follow Steps 1 to 4 on page 14 to prepare the fabric for dyeing. Number the pieces of fabric from #1 through #11 prior to soaking.

2. Line up your cups and measure dye into them according to the formulae on the chart (Figure 5-1). You will notice that there are no formulae for the last four cups. That is because we want you

Cup #1
2 tablespoons of red
2 tablespoons of blue
2 tablespoons of yellow

Cup #2
1 tablespoon of red
1 tablespoon of blue
2 tablespoons of yellow

Cup #3
1 tablespoon of red
2 tablespoons of blue
1 tablespoon of yellow

Cup #4
4 tablespoons of red
1 tablespoon of blue
1 tablespoon of yellow

Cup #5
1 tablespoon of red
2 tablespoons of blue
2 tablespoons of yellow

Cup #6
2 tablespoons of red
1 tablespoon of blue
3 tablespoons of yellow

Cup #7
3 tablespoons of red
2 tablespoons of blue
2 tablespoons of yellow

Cup #8   **Cup #9**   **Cup #10**   **Cup #11**

Figure 5.1

Mixing Chart to Create Neutrals from Primaries

to begin to experiment. You can either write down the your new formulae, or you can just consider them random dye colors that you won't be able to repeat.

3. Dye the fabrics, following the basic steps for the cup method in Workshop 1.2.

4. Allow the fabric to cure and then rinse, wash, dry, and iron.

RESULTS

These are lovely earth-tone colors. Several of them, #1, #2, #3, and #5, would be wonderful neutral backgrounds when dyed in even lighter values. The proportion of dye powder per cup of water was altered from the normal base solution provided in Chapter 1. And a different primary red (scarlet) was substituted for fuchsia. If you are willing to experiment, you can dye all kinds of unique colors. Use Record Sheet #4 (Appendix 1) to record the results of this Workshop.

VARIATION

Neutralized colors that harmonize with your color scheme can be made by mixing together any two colors contained in the scheme. A color run between the two main colors in your color scheme will usually provide the right neutralized color for your quilt. Study the new hues in the color run to find the ones you like best, then make value gradations for it. You will have a perfect neutral that will make your quilt come to life.

Neutralizing Primaries to Create Neutrals (Cups #1 to #7 only)

Method: Cup method

Time: 30 minutes

Fabric: 9 pieces, each approx.
⅛ yard (12 cm)

Dye Powders: 2 teaspoons of black for
Set #1

1 teaspoon of black for
Set #2

1 teaspoon of brown for
Set #3

¾ teaspoon of red

1½ teaspoons of blue

2¼ teaspoons of yellow

Equipment: 5 plastic cups

5 plastic spoons

Measuring cup

Measuring spoons

This project gives you very grayed, neutralized primary colors. The first set will be neutralized with a strong black, the second with a weaker black, and the third with a brown dye solution. You can use any dye powder, not just primaries, for this Workshop.

1. Follow Steps 1-4 on page 14 to prepare the fabric for dyeing.
2. For Set #1, mix 2 teaspoons of black dye powder with ½ cup (4 oz) warm water; mix the three primary colors each with ¾ cup (6 oz) warm water.
3. Follow Figure 5.2 for the proportions of black to primary color. Dye three pieces of fabric in the black mixture, using the cup method as described in Step 5 on pages 14-15. The mottled textures you will get are beautiful and add an extra dimension to neutral fabrics.
4. For Set #2, mix 1 teaspoon of black dye powder with ½ cup (4 oz) warm water. Again following Figure 5.2 as a guide to the proportions of black to primary color, dye three pieces of fabric. This time, you

Set #1

Cup #1
1 tablespoon water
2 tablespoons of black
½ tablespoon of red

Cup #2
1 tablespoon water
2 tablespoons of black
½ tablespoon of yellow

Cup #3
1 tablespoon water
2 tablespoons of black
½ tablespoon of blue

Set #2

Cup #4
1 tablespoon water
2 tablespoons of black
1½ tablespoon of red

Cup #5
1 tablespoon water
2 tablespoons of black
1½ tablespoon of yellow

Cup #6
1 tablespoon water
2 tablespoons of black
1½ tablespoon of blue

Set #3

Cup #7
1 tablespoon water
2 tablespoons of brown
½ tablespoon of red

Cup #8
1 tablespoon water
2 tablespoons of brown
½ tablespoon of yellow

Cup #9
1 tablespoon water
2 tablespoons of brown
½ tablespoon of blue

Figure 5.2

Mixing Chart for Neutralizing Primary Colors with Black or Brown

are using a weaker black solution and three times as much primary color.

5. For Set #3, repeat Step 4, with the brown dye powder and the primaries, again dyeing three pieces of fabric.

6. Allow the fabric to cure, then rinse, wash, dry, and iron.

RESULTS

Lay out the nine fabric samples side by side, grouped according to blacks and browns. Study them to see the changes from on to the next. Notice what happens when the solution is stronger and less primary color is used. Your final color is darker and more neutral. If you use as a primary color a claret that is already a grayed or neutralized color, the results will be very different than with brighter primaries. Use Record Sheet #4: Color Test Results (Appendix 1) to record the results of this Workshop.

Tip: Because the colors you dye will be so dark, you cannot label your fabric pieces with a marker. Use safety pins instead. On a corner of fabric piece #1, put a large safety pin. Use a small safety pin on piece #2. Piece #3 gets a tiny brass safety pin, and so on. One piece could have no pin. Make a note of your code, so you will remember which piece you put in which cup: you will then be able to complete a record sheet.

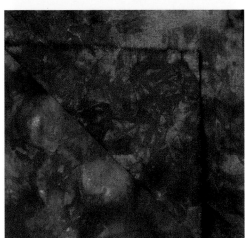

Neutralizing Primary Colors (top left) with Black (top right—Set #1—and bottom left—Set #2) and Brown (bottom right—Set #3)

SPECIAL TECHNIQUES

No matter how confident you become with hand dyeing, there will always be times when you dye fabric colors that you do not like or when you find pieces of fabric in your stash that no longer appeal to you. You will also find that, for some quilts, neither solid colors nor the mottled effect is what you are looking for. Sometimes you just want stronger or more unusual color variations on a piece of fabric. This chapter shows you how, once you are comfortable working with dyes, you can try out techniques that will give your quilts that one-of-a-kind look.

Just Strips
30½" x 30½" (77 cm x 77 cm)
Designed and sewn by Joyce Mori
Darker saturated colors are strip-pieced together and then cut into triangles. Two triangles
form a square. A lovely gray neutral is used for the sashing and borders to set off the strip-pieced
units. Since the strips can be any width, this is a great quilt to make from scraps.

Tip: Dye a small sample of fabric to check the results before you overdye large pieces

OVERDYEING FABRICS

Overdyeing is the process of re-dyeing fabric that has previously been hand- or commercially dyed, in order to alter the color. The direct-dyeing techniques on which this book are based provide a wonderful way to overdye your fabrics, so that you may achieve changes in value, chroma, and hue. For instance, it can be difficult to use a dark fabric that has areas of white in it. The eye is drawn to the lighter areas as a focal point and not to the overall design of the quilt. By overdying this fabric you can darken it so that the white is less intrusive.

Colors created from dyes are transparent. You can use overdyeing to bring about different colors; you can also make different values of the original color. For example, if you overdye a yellow fabric with blue dye, you will change the color of the fabric to green. Also, if you overdye a bright orange with its complement, blue, you will change that color to a darker value, a duller orange. Consult the mixing formulae and color runs given in Chapters 3 and 4 for help in determining which colors to choose to achieve the desired results. Workshop 6.1 explains how to overdye a color with its complement.

A fabric with a commercially printed design will not be completely covered by overdyeing. The background accepts the dye to a greater extent than the print. For example, if your fabric is printed with black on a light pink background, then overdyed with a medium-value blue, the background will become a shade of violet, but the dark print will become only slightly darker and take on a bluish cast.

Commercially available tone-on-tone prints found in white and beige are an excellent choice for overdyeing, because the background takes the dye well but the printed design does not change. This is an easy way to get a hand-dyed patterned fabric in exactly the color you want.

If you want to unify many diverse printed fabrics so you can use them in a quilt, you can overdye them with the same color. The resulting fabrics will blend well together. Some quilters like to overdye with a beige dye to lend an aged or antique look to the fabrics.

A fabric cannot be changed to a lighter color by overdyeing; you can only deepen the color. Light- to medium-colored fabrics are the most suitable for overdyeing. You can overdye with a darker shade of the original color or with a light-to-medium value of black dye solution. If you choose to dye with a different color, the original color of the fabric and the choice of dye color must be carefully thought out to achieve the results you are after. For example, overdyeing a dark- or medium-value green with a pale yellow will only make the green a little more yellowish, but overdyeing a pale yellow in a medium value of green with the cup method will give you a yellow-green fabric with highlights of yellow showing through.

A great way to achieve multi-colored fabrics is by using the cup method to overdye a fabric one or more times. The scrunching of the fabric into the cup prevents the overdye color from completely covering all the original color of the fabric. The original color will show through in some areas. You might want to heighten the

GANADO
31" x 27" (79 cm x 69 cm)
Designed, sewn, and hand-quilted by Joyce Mori
More than ten different red dye powders were used to dye the red fabrics. These were
overdyed with black to create more variations. The design is adapted from the
Streak of Lightning block, Navajo rugs, and an ethnic pillow design.

effect by deliberately pushing the fabric very compactly into the cup, especially if you overdye the same fabric several times. You would want to have some areas of each hue stay unaltered by succeeding solutions.

Transparent effects, those in which one color appears to overlap the other, are easily accomplished with overdyeing. Start with the lighter hue and overdye with a light-to-medium value dye solution of the second color. The illusion of overlapping fabrics may be seen the quilt on page 96, in which some of the red-violet and dark green fabrics in the borders were overdyed with a medium value of blue-violet, and the grayed-green background and the neutral gray border fabric were overdyed with the darker green.

Almost any fabric can be overdyed in black, navy, or brown. Your new color will be a black, navy or brown that has a leaning towards the original color, especially if you are working with hand-dyed fabrics. For instance, overdyeing a blue with a black will give you a fabric that is bluish-black. These dark colors are particular helpful for treating fabric "disasters." Overdye them, whether ugly solids or unattractive prints, with any of the above-mentioned colors and see if they do not become a usable part of your fabric stash.

When deciding whether or not a fabric is a suitable candidate for overdyeing, use the same guidelines as for choosing a fabric for dyeing. Remember that all-cotton fabric works best; if you overdye a cotton blend, only the cotton fibers will absorb the dye, yielding a not-unattractive heather-like appearance. And, although it is best

Tip: When making transparent effects, it is a good idea to overdye several pieces of fabric, making more value gradations than you think you will need. You then have several fabrics to select from when choosing the ones that achieve the best transparent effect.

to avoid fabric with finishes on them, commercially printed fabric can usually be successfully overdyed.

OTHER SPECIAL TECHNIQUES

The dyeing techniques you have learned are very versatile, and you will surely find many ways to adapt the basic methods to create unusual, often one-of-a-kind fabrics. You should make it a practice, as we do, to set aside time each month to try new ideas. The results you get from experimenting are often unpredictable and are always interesting. Many times the outcome from the first test of an idea will make you re-think and modify the technique, then try it in a revised way for better results. Think of your experiments as offering you new ways to manipulate the dye, as offering you the opportunity to be an inventor.

The ideas in Workshops 6.2 to 6.5 were adapted from other dyeing, fabric painting, and art techniques. They produce patterned fabrics that make unusual combinations with other hand-dyed or commercial fabrics. They can add visual variety to that special quilt you design and sew.

Carefully read the instructions with each Workshop, because they sometimes have very specific requirements. Some of them are messy, so consider them for a backyard, garage, or basement activity.

WHAT'S NEXT?

In the next chapter, we will show you how to use new "rules" for color mixing just to please yourself and to have fun with color.

70

OLIVE JAR MANIA
28" x 28" (71 cm x 71 cm)
Designed and sewn by Joyce Mori; hand-quilted by Delores Stemple, Aurora, WV
These dye patterns were created by placing a folded fabric in a glass olive jar.
The resulting fabrics are wild, graphic, and beautifully patterned. To provide contrast,
very pale fabrics were used to complete each block.

Method: Bowl method

Time: 10 minutes

Fabric: ⅛ yard (12 cm) of fabric. To work with larger pieces of fabric, increase the water and dye proportionately (see Appendix 2)

Dye Solution: ¼ cup (2 oz) in a complement to the fabric

One of the easiest ways to change the color of a fabric is to overdye it with its complement. The color will be dulled, or reduced in intensity, as you remember from the projects in Chapter 4. You need only a small amount of dye color to make a noticeable change in the original fabric color, so you should begin by using a diluted dye solution. You can always re-dye if the change is not enough to suit you.

1. Follow Steps 1-4 on page 14 to prepare the fabric for dyeing.
2. First, locate on the color wheel the nearest match you can find to the color you want to change. Next, find its complement by seeking the color opposite it on the color wheel.
3. Mix a dye solution for the complementary color following the color wheel recipe, then make a light value by adding approximately ½ teaspoon of dye solution to ¼ cup (2 oz) water.
4. Dye the fabric according to the directions in Workshop 1.1.
5. Allow the fabric to cure and then rinse, wash, dry and iron.

RESULTS

This principle of overdyeing with a complement works for any color you wish to change by darkening or dulling.

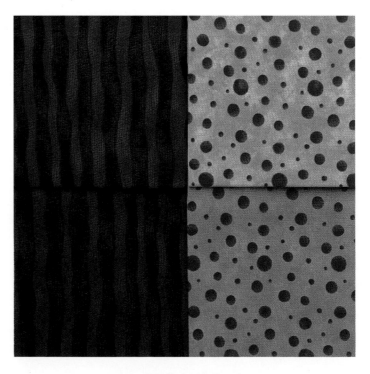

Fabrics Overdyed with Complements

WORKSHOP 6.2 IMITATION TIE DYE

The fabric design made in this project is reminiscent of tie dye, but there is no need to tie off the fabric. The secret is a bottle or jar approximately 6" (15 cm) high and 1¾" (4.5 cm) in diameter—the size used for olives. Note to, that you are using a fat quarter of fabric rather than the usual fat eighth.

1. Follow Steps 1-4 on page 14 to prepare the fabric for dyeing.
2. With fabric on a flat surface, accordion-fold it into 1" (2.5 cm) pleats. (The pleats do not have to be perfect.)
3. Pour ⅛ cup (1 oz) of dye solution in the jar. Fold the pleated fabric in half, ends together, and carefully push it down into the jar with the dowel. The fabric will be longer than the jar, but continue pushing it with the dowel until it is all fitted into the jar. It will probably be an inch or so from the top. Add more dye solution if needed to cover the fabric.
4. Allow the fabric to cure, and then rinse, wash, dry and iron.

RESULTS

You will notice that the tighter you push the fabric into the jar, the less the dye is able to penetrate the fabric and color it. After you do one piece, you will be able to determine if you want less patterning, i.e., by making the fabric tighter in the jar. This fabric has specific design repeat. You can use it much like border or striped fabric.

Time:	5 minutes
Fabric:	Fat quarter, 18" x 22" (46 cm x 56 cm)
Dye Solution:	⅛ cup (1 oz), any color
Equipment:	Bottle or jar 12" (30.5 cm) wooden dowel

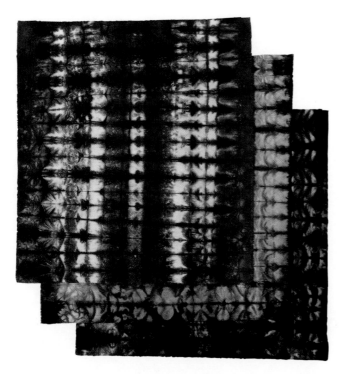

Imitation Tie-dye

Time: 10 minutes

Fabric: Fat eighths (23 cm x 56 cm)
               or fat quarters (46 cm x
               56 cm)

Dye Solution: ¼ cup (2 oz) of any two
               colors

Equipment: 2 bowls about 6" to 8" (15
               cm to 20 cm) in diameter

Using a patterned fabric in a quilt can add interest to the design. This wavy stripe fabric is lovely. It can tie together the other colors selected for the quilt very effectively.

1. Follow Steps 1-4 on page 14 to prepare the fabric for dyeing. Pour each dye solution into a bowl.
2. Accordion-fold the fabric in 1" (2.5 cm) pleats. Fold it into thirds to fit into the bowl. Dip one long side of the folded pleats into one of the bowls of dye. Hold the fabric in the liquid for a couple of seconds, then lift it out of the dye and let the excess drain back into the bowl.
3. Dip the other long side of the folded fabric into the second color dye solution, holding for a few seconds, then draining as before.
4. Place the fabric in a plastic bag to cure, flattening it out but still folded to keep the colors separate.
5. Rinse, wash, dry, and iron.

RESULTS

The two-color stripes are not straight and crisp, but provide an interesting and useful patterned fabric.

Two-colored Stripes

WORKSHOP 6.4 DYE POWDER BURSTS

This is a somewhat messy technique, and it should be done outside or in an area where drips and splashes won't be a problem. Dye as much fabric as you think you will use, as this is not a procedure you are likely to do every day. If you work outside, choose a day that is not so hot, dry and windy that the fabric will dry too quickly. Be sure to wear your mask.

1. Follow Steps 1-4 on page 14 to prepare the fabric for dyeing. Put the dye powder in the salt shaker.
2. Lay the damp fabric flat. Sprinkle the dye powder randomly on the surface. The particles of the dye powder will make colorful bursts as they touch the damp fabric.
3. Hang the fabric on the clothesline and spray it with the soaking liquid. Allow it to hang for several minutes so the dye will run down the fabric.
4. When the dye has stopped running, place the fabric in a plastic bag to cure.
5. Allow the fabric to cure, and then rinse, wash, dry and iron.

RESULTS

The fabric looks like fireworks falling down from the sky, streaks of color cascading from a focal point of color.

VARIATION

For a more controlled result, sprinkle the dye powder on the damp fabric, as many colors as you like, as many dots as you like, but place the fabric directly into a plastic bag rather than hanging it on a clothesline. Allow the fabric to cure in the plastic bag, then rinse, wash, dry, and iron it. Compare the results to your first experiment with dry dye powder.

Time:	10 minutes
Fabric:	As desired
Dye Powder:	½ teaspoon, any color
Equipment:	Temporary clothesline
	Salt shaker or homemade substitute
	Small spray bottle filled with soaking solution

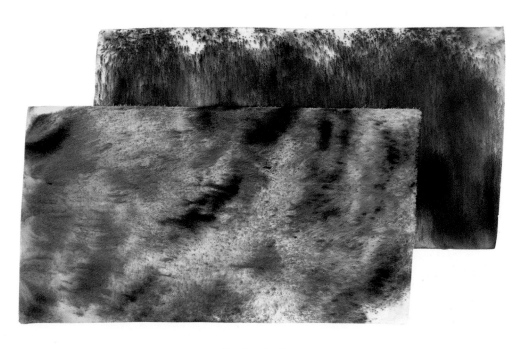

Dye Powder Bursts

Workshop 6.5 Striping a Fabric with Different Value Gradations

Time:	20 minutes
Fabric:	Fat eights (23 cm x 56 cm) or fat quarters (46 cm x 56 cm)
Dye Solution:	½ cup (4 oz), any color
Equipment:	Four 1" (2.5 cm) foam brushes 4 plastic cups Layer of paper towels on your work surface to soak up extra dye liquid

Different values of a color are used to make subtle stripes for a lovely tone-on-tone look. An alternative to using four values of a single color is to use a series of different colors. An interesting fabric for binding your quilts can be made by cutting across the stripes.

1. Follow steps 1-4 on page 14 to prepare the fabric for dyeing. Allow the fabric to air dry, and iron it flat if wrinkled.
2. Fill the cups according to Figure 6.1.
3. Using the foam brush, apply the dye solution from cup #1 in a 2" (5 cm) wide stripe across the fabric. Paint a second stripe below the first one, using the solution from cup #2. Continue with cups #3 and #4. Start over with cup #1 and paint stripes from each cup until the entire fabric is covered.
4. Keep the fabric flat and allow it to cure in a plastic bag. When it has finished curing, rinse, wash, dry and iron.

Results

This value gradation shows all four gradations on a single piece of fabric.

Cup #1
⅛ cup of dye solution

Cup #2
⅛ cup of water
2 teaspoons of dye solution

Cup #3
⅛ cup of water
1 teaspoon of dye solution

Cup #4
⅛ cup of water
½ teaspoon of dye solution

Figure 6.1
Mixing Chart for Striped Fabrics

Tonal Stripes

CREATIVITY AND COLOR PLAY

IT IS ONLY IN CREATIVE WORK THAT JOY MAY BE FOUND.
—Robert Henri, *The Art Spirit*

So far, *Dyeing to Quilt* has explained systematic methods of mixing colors. The primary advantage of such controlled mixing is that colors can be exactly duplicated time and again, using the standardized formulae that are the heart of this color system. However, as you gain experience, you may find yourself wanting to break away from the system from time to time. By simply playing with the dyes, mixing whatever you have at hand to see what happens, you can learn a lot—while having fun. Color play gives you lovely fabrics that add an unusual touch to any quilt.

The Child in All of Us
27" x 27" (69 cm x 69 cm)
Designed, sewn, and hand-quilted by Pat Hill, West Hills, CA
There are two sets of analogous colors in this quilt. One is centered on red; the other on green.
Because these colors are complements, the quilt has visual impact. The colors were not dyed
in a single dye run, yet they still combine effectively.

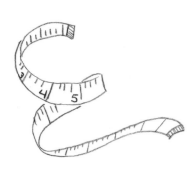

• When you hand-dye fabrics, you are creating. Think of changing the color of a piece of fabric as a means of self expression. These are *your* colors.

• To be creative means you must take risks. As with any other new skill, be willing to explore the potential of fabric dyeing. Keep experimenting. Allow yourself the creative freedom to mix any colors. Try new dye powders; there is no one "right" formula or set of dyes.

• Don't be afraid of failure, because you can't fail. With dyes you can overdye a mistake with another color. As a last resort you can always dye your fabric black! Much better, use the unusual colors you make—no matter how unappealing they seem at first—in a quilt. This is a wonderful way to stretch your imagination as a quilter.

• Keep dyeing—you just may find there is nothing more fun to do. The sense of accomplishment and satisfaction you feel will become addictive. Soon you will eagerly anticipate your dyeing session, whether it's a 15-minute quickie or a more satisfying 2-hour project. You may be working at dyeing fabric, but you are playing with color.

• Stay focused on the process. When you dye, concentrate on the act of dyeing and how the colors interact. Put your energies into what you are doing and tune everything else out.

• Visualize the results. As you dye, think of the wonderful quilts you will be able to make with your new fabrics. Seeing your own lovely hand-dyed fabrics in your own quilts is the most satisfying experience you will have as a quilter.

• Have faith in yourself. "There is nothing better than that a man should rejoice his own works." Ecclesiastics 3:22

RANDOM MIXING

Random mixing is exactly as it sounds—mixing any dye solutions together, in any order, and in any proportions you please. Once you begin to hand-dye your own fabrics, you quickly find that you have several small amounts of different dye solutions left after each of your dyeing sessions. Instead of throwing left-over dye solution away, save it for random mixing. Dye solutions that have been sitting in the refrigerator are also ideal for random mixing.

To begin random mixing, just set up a group of cups in which to mix your solutions and stuff your fabric. This is the time to mix colors together that you have not tried before. Try putting two colors together without mixing the solution before you dye the fabrics. Add the complements or black to any colors. Make some lighter values of the colors. As you will see, you can have fun with your dyeing while learning about the nature of many dye colors. The Workshops in this chapter will give you ideas on experimenting with dyes to help you get started.

CHANGING A DYE COLOR

Perhaps you have a dye powder whose color you do not particularly like. By mixing it with other dyes, you can easily change it. Look what happened when we decided to mix an unappealing bronze dye with each of the three primary colors— red, blue, and yellow.

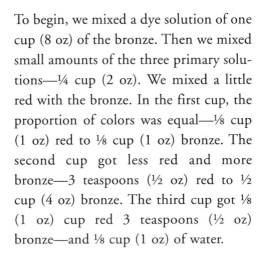

Nine Fabrics Mixed From Bronze

To begin, we mixed a dye solution of one cup (8 oz) of the bronze. Then we mixed small amounts of the three primary solutions—¼ cup (2 oz). We mixed a little red with the bronze. In the first cup, the proportion of colors was equal—⅛ cup (1 oz) red to ⅛ cup (1 oz) bronze. The second cup got less red and more bronze—3 teaspoons (½ oz) red to ½ cup (4 oz) bronze. The third cup got ⅛ (1 oz) cup red 3 teaspoons (½ oz) bronze—and ⅛ cup (1 oz) of water.

We did the same thing with the blue and yellow dye solutions, so that when we were done, we had nine new colors.

WHAT'S NEXT?

You are now ready to sew your own quilting projects. You have acquired a good, basic knowledge of the rules of color, and you now know how to step outside the rules to make unusual and unique colors of your own. Even the most traditional quilt patterns will take on new looks with your own special hand-dyed fabrics, in colors only you could have imagined—or hit on by accident. Your quilt making will never be the same—you have graduated to a higher level of creativity! The final chapter provides patterns for six quilts that are ideal for using hand-dyed fabrics.

SCRAPS—LIGHT AND DARK
33" x 33" (84 cm x 84 cm)
Designed and sewn by Joyce Mori; machine-quilted by Theresa Fleming of Aurora, CO
A variety of fabrics in light and dark values was used to create this quilt. The wide range of
colors makes this an ideal project for hand-dyed fabrics.

WORKSHOP 7.1 A TWO-COLOR DYE RUN WITH RANDOM DYES

For this quick and easy Workshop, use any colors—primaries or mixed—that you happen to have or about which you are curious. Though you can use the bowl method, we recommend the cup method because of the mottled texture of the colors you achieve, and because it is a simpler process.

1. Follow Steps 1-4 on page 14 to prepare the fabric for dyeing.

2. Set out a group of cups, at least ten. Mix one cup (8 oz) of dye solution for each of the two colors you are using. Use the following recipes: for colors in the red, orange or violet families, use 1 teaspoon of dye powder per cup (8 oz) of water; for blue or green colors, use 2 teaspoons of dye powder per cup (8 oz) of water; and for yellow or black, use 3 teaspoons of dye powder per cup (8 oz) of water.

3. Fill the cups following the chart in Figure 7-l. The chart is meant only as a guide; experiment with any proportions of dye solution-to-water you wish.

4. Dye the fabric, using the cup method (see Workshop 1.2). Alternatively use one of these variations:

(a) Do not mix the dye colors before adding the fabric. If you simply pour the solutions into the cup, then immerse the fabric, you will obtain more marbling and more nuances of color. The effect can be striking.

(b) Pour one color of dye into the cup. Stuff the fabric halfway into the cup, then add the second color of dye and push the remainder of the fabric in. The fabric often turns out half in one color and half the other, with a mixed color in the middle.

(c) For an unusual, multi-color effect, pour one of your dye solutions into a shallow container, such as a frozen desert bowl, then place the unfolded fabric in the dye. Add the second dye color by pouring it over the fabric. Not all of the fabric will be covered with dye. You can push it into the dye if you wish.

5. Allow the fabric to cure in the dye, then rinse, wash, dry, and iron.

RESULTS

Don't be concerned if all your colors are not sharply distinguished from each other. You can pull those fabrics out, saving them in your fabric stash until the perfect quilting project comes along where you can use them for special effects.

Method:	Cup method
Time:	15-20 minutes
Fabric:	10 pieces, each approx. ⅛ yard (12 cm)
Dye Solution:	1 cup (8 oz) each of two colors
Equipment:	10 or more plastic cups

Tip: To preview a color, put a drop of the dye solution on a piece of white paper, then wipe it off with a paper towel. The color remaining on the white paper is a reasonable approximation of the final color you will achieve after the fabric is rinsed, washed, and dried. The color of the dye solution in the cup is not a good indication.

Cup #1
4 tablespoons of water
1 tablespoon of Color A

Cup #2
4 tablespoons of water
1½ teaspoons of Color A

Cup #3
2 tablespoons of water
2 tablespoons of Color A

Cup #4
2 tablespoons of Color A
2 tablespoons of Color B

Cup #5
1 tablespoon of Color A
6 tablespoons of Color B

Cup #6
6 tablespoons of Color A
1 tablespoon of Color B

Cup #7
1½ teaspoons of Color A
6 tablespoons of Color B

Cup #8
4 tablespoons of water
1 tablespoon of Color B

Cup #9
4 tablespoons of water
1½ teaspoons of Color B

Cup #10
2 tablespoons of water
2 tablespoons of Color B

Figure 7.1

Mixing Chart for a Two-Color Dye Run with Random Colors

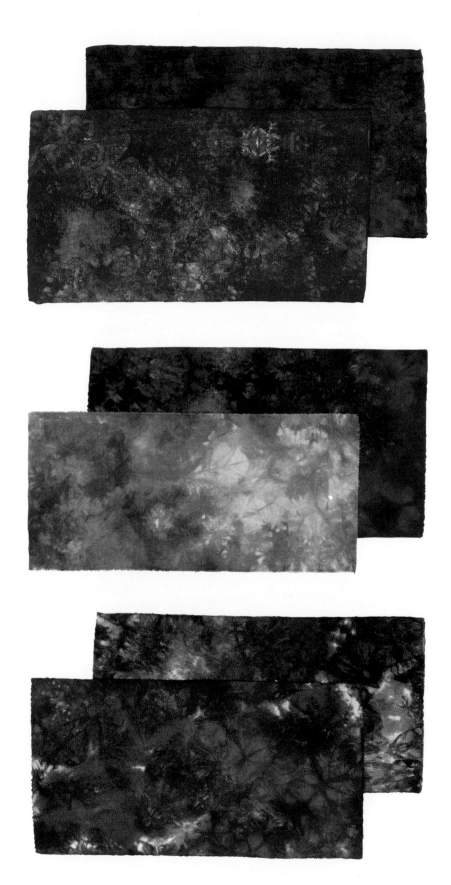

From Top: Variation A, Variation B and Variation C

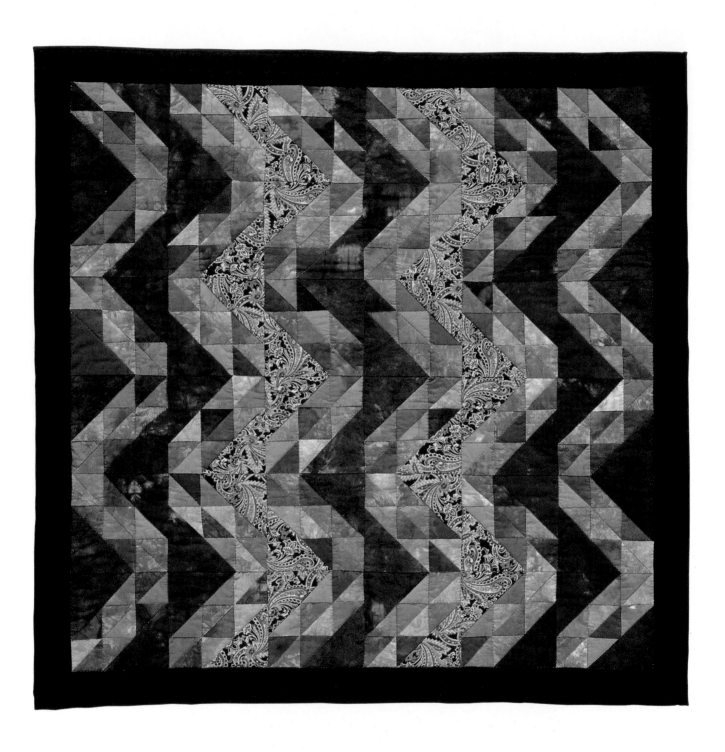

SPARKLING LIGHTS
37½" x 37½" (95 cm x 95 cm)
Designed, sewn, and hand-quilted by Joyce Mori
The same block design is used in Fall Comes to Michigan on page 57. Many of the light
colors in this quilt are neutralized colors so they are soft and subtle. Even so, they still
stand out against the dark values in the quilt.

WORKSHOP 7.2 RANDOM VALUES

In previous Workshops, you practiced very precise ways to control value differences and gradations in colors. Here, there is no control—we want you to just have fun playing with values. Though you can creates random values with the cup method, for this Workshop we recommend the bowl method, as the value differences are easier to see.

1. Follow Steps 1-4 on page 14 to prepare the fabric for dyeing.
2. Pour different amounts of water into each of four cups—no water in the first, ¼ cup (2 oz) in the second, ½ cup (4 oz) in the third, and 1 cup (8 oz in the last). Pour ¼ cup (2 oz) of dye solution into the first cup, and a tablespoon of dye solution into the other three.
3. Dye the fabrics, using the bowl method (see Workshop 1.1).
4. Allow the fabric to cure, then rinse, wash, dry, and iron.

RESULTS
The Workshop creates dark to light versions of a color. Try repeating using the cup method for more subtle value differences.

Method:	Bowl method
Time:	10 minutes or more, depending on the number of values you select
Fabric:	Four ⅛ yard (12 cm) pieces per color
Dye Solution:	½ cup (4 oz), any color
Equipment:	4 plastic cups
	4 plastic bags

Random Dyeing

CHAPTER 8

QUILTS TO DYE FOR

These six projects are designed to show you how to plan a quilt that uses hand-dyed fabrics. You will find quilts that take advantage of the transparent looks that can be achieved with dyed fabrics; others will emphasize a colorwash effect by using many different values of a hue; still others will show the versatility of toned and neutralized hues. We hope you will use the techniques in *Dyeing to Quilt* to dye fabrics for your own quilts. Even more, we hope you will experiment and develop your own ideas.

Note: All templates include seam allowances, unless stated otherwise.

CHRISTMAS VALUES
26" x 26" (66 cm x 66 cm)
Designed and sewn by Joyce Mori; hand-quilted by Delores Stemple, Aurora, WV
Red and green in several values are combined in this rotary cut quilt. The centers
of each block are of the neutral values formed when red and green dyes are mixed
in different proportions in several cups.

Block Size: 6" (15.2 cm)

Setting: 20 blocks, set 4 by 5

Fabric: ⅜ yard (34 cm) each of four values of gray

⅛ yard (12 cm) each of six values of red

⅛ yard (12 cm) of each of six values of violet

Cutting: Template A: 10 of each value of gray

Sashing strips: 15 red, 16 violet cut to 2½" x 6½" (6.4 cm x 16.5 cm) See step 2, below

Connecting squares: 12 each of 2½" x 2½" (6.4 cm x 6.4 cm) in two dark values of violet

Binding: ¼ yard (23 cm)

Backing: 1 yard (1 meter)

This quilt was inspired by the over-under woven lattice quilts of Miriam Nathan Roberts. Gradations, dyed in a random technique (see Workshop 7.2) using the cup method, were used to make the sashing strips for the blocks. Check Appendix 2 for the formulae to mix larger quantities of dye solution.

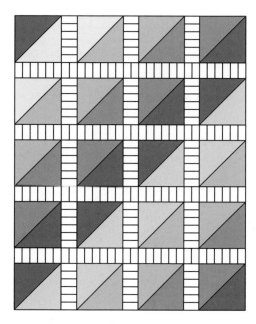

Figure 8.1

1. Sew two Template A triangles together to form the squares that make up the body of the quilt. Use Figure 8.1 to determine color combinations.

2. Make the sashing units by strip-piecing the six values of red together so that the darkest reds are at the center (see Figure 8.2). For the violets, place the lightest values at the center of the strip. Each strip is cut 1½" (3.8 cm) wide. When the unit of six strips is sewn, slice off sections that are 2½" (6.4 cm) wide, including seam allowances.

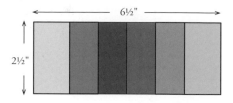

Figure 8.2

3. Make the connecting squares by strip-piecing the two dark values of violet together, then cutting twelve 2½" (6.4 cm) squares from the strip.

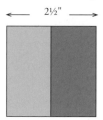

Figure 8.3

3. Using Figure 8.1 as a guide, sort the squares into pairs, and join each pair with a red sashing strip. Then, sew the two pairs of each row together, placing a red sashing strip between each.

4. To make the horizontal sashing strips that go between the rows, sew a corner square between two violet sashing strips. Join two pairs of sashing strips with another corner square. Make a total of four units that consist of four sashing strips and three corner squares.

5. Sew the rows together, placing a strip of violet horizontal sashing between each row. Take care to get each row of squares going in the right direction.

6. Make a quilt "sandwich" of backing, batting, and quilt top; thread- or pin-baste. Quilt as desired. Bind and label your quilt.

Gray Gradation
30" x 38" (76 cm by 96.5 cm)
Designed, sewn, and hand-quilted by Joyce Mori
Value gradations dyed with a random technique were used for the blocks and the
sashing strips. The cup method gives the quilt its wonderful mottled fabrics.

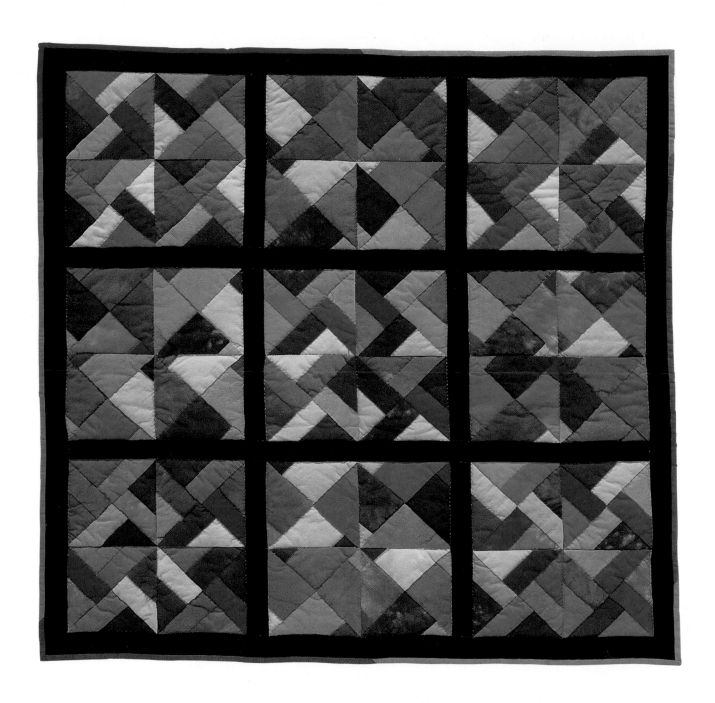

COLORFUL PINWHEELS
28" x 28" (71 cm by 71 cm)
Designed and sewn by Joyce Mori; hand-quilted by Delores Stemple, Aurora, WV
As your fabric stash expands, you will need to find quilt designs that use a variety of unusual
colors that may be left over from other quilts. This scrap quilt does just that.

This scrap quilt, made up of strips of many different fabrics, is wonderful in hand-dyed fabric. It is a natural for unusual colors that might be difficult to place. The quilt works up quickly, as each piece can be easily strip-pieced and rotary-cut.

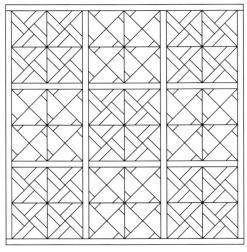

Figure 8.4

1. Sew a narrow (1½"/3.8 cm) and a wide (2½"/6.4 cm) strip of any two colors together lengthwise. Place Template A on the strip and mark as shown in Figure 8.5. Notice that you cut two same-size triangles, A and B. You will need 80 of triangle A and 64 of triangle B.

2½"

1½"

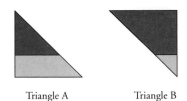

Triangle A   Triangle B

Figure 8.5

2. Sew 4 Template A triangles to make a pinwheel unit. Sew 4 of these together to complete a block, as in Figure 8.6. Make 5 blocks from A triangles and 4 from B triangles (see Figure 8.7).

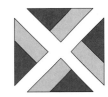

Figure 8.6

Block A

Block B

Figure 8.7

3. Lay out the blocks as shown in Figure 8.4. Sew the short sashing strips between them to make rows. Sew the long sashing strips between the rows as you join them to make the quilt top. Trim, as necessary. Sew on the borders.
4. Make a quilt "sandwich" of backing batting, and quilt top, thread- or pin-baste. Quilt as desired. Bind and label.

Block Size:	8½" (21.6 cm)
Setting:	9 blocks, set 3 by 3
Fabric:	Scraps in several fabrics, totalling up to 1 yard (1 meter)
	¼ yard (23 cm) of black for sashing and borders
Cutting:	144 triangle units
	Sashing strips: Six 1½" x 9½" (3.8 cm x 24.1 cm); two 1½" x 28" (3.8 cm x 71.1 cm)
Borders:	Four 1½" x 30" (3.8 cm x 76.2 cm) strips
Binding:	¼ yard (23 cm)
Backing:	1 yard (1 meter)

Block Size: 6" (15.2 cm)

Setting: 4 blocks, set 2 by 2

Fabric: Dark green: Fat quarter (9" x 22"/23 cm x 56 cm)

Medium green: ⅛ yard (12 cm)

Light green: Fat quarter (9" x 22"/23 cm x 56 cm)

Red: Fat quarter (9" x 22"/23 cm x 56 cm)

Lilac: ⅛ yard (12 cm)

Cutting: Template A: 4 each dark green, light green, red, and lilac

Template B: 8 medium green; 40 light green; 48 red; 8 lilac

Template C: 4 each medium green, red, and lilac

Template D: 4 lilac

Template E: 4 light green

Template F: 4 each light green and red

Template G: Four in red

Template H: 1 dark green

Borders: In dark green, 2 strips of 1½" x 14½" (3.8 cm x 36.8 cm) and 2 strips of 1½" x 16½" (3.8 x 41.9 cm)

Binding: ⅛ yard (12 cm)

Backing: Fat quarter (18" x 22"/46 cm x 56 cm)

This quilt sparkles because of the interplay between complementary colors dyed using the cup and bowl methods. Three values of green provide contrast with each other and with the red. Figure 8-8 shows how this little quilt is put together. Pieced sashing strips run through the center to divide it into four squares. You will piece each of the four squares, then sew them together after you have pieced the sashing.

Figure 8.8

1. Begin by sewing the Template B triangles together to form 8 squares of lilac/red and 40 of light green/red. Piece the 8 lilac/medium green squares for the central sashing.

2. Working from the center and in the bottom right square, sew a lilac and a dark green square together; add a lilac Template C to the AA edge. Then sew a lilac/red square to a red square and add it to the AAC unit. Keep building up the block by working out from the center. Use Figure 8.9 as a guide. As you reach

the outer edge, make a pieced border of red/light green squares that meet in the corner with a light green square. Make three more blocks.

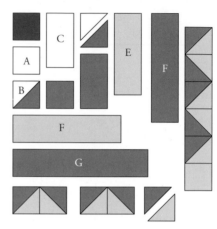

Figure 8.9

3. Piece 4 sashing strips. Sew one to either side of central square H.

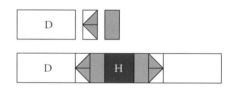

Figure 8.10

4. Sew a block to either side of the remaining 2 sashing strips. You now have 2 rows of 2 blocks and 1 sashing strip. Sew the rows to either side of the long sashing strip with the central square.

5. Add the outer borders after first measuring correctly across the center of the quilt. Pin the borders in place and stitch after making sure they fit. Trim away any excess length.

6. Make a quilt "sandwich" of backing, batting, and quilt top; thread- or pin-baste. Quilt as desired. Bind and label.

CHRISTMAS MINIATURE
16" x 16" (41 cm by 41 cm)
Designed, sewn, and hand-quilted by Joyce Mori
Three values of green with a complement of red add sparkle and intensity to
this miniature quilt design. Quick and easy to complete, this little quilt is perfect
for busy hands before Christmas.

AMAZING GRAPES
35½" x 35½" (90 cm x 90 cm)
Designed, machine-pieced and hand-quilted by Cynthia Myerberg
The grape-basket blocks are set on point and bordered by bands of color. These bands
appear to be transparent when they overlap the borders of the larger square. The illusion of
transparency was achieved by overdyeing a color with the color that it overlaps.

A traditional basket block, repeated four times, is the focus of this square-within-a-square wall quilt. The baskets are set on point and bordered by bands of color that appear to be laid on top of one another. The use of analogous colors and the technique of overdyeing are the secrets to creating this illusion of transparency. The neutral background and border colors were dyed by first doing a color run between violet and a shade of green. Then, several lighter values of a neutral gray/green selected from the color run were dyed.

Figure 8.11

1. To prepare strips E, H, F, and K so that the corners can be mitered, place the miter guide as shown Figure 8.12. Cut along the diagonal edge with a rotary cutter. Reverse the miter guide for use at the other end.

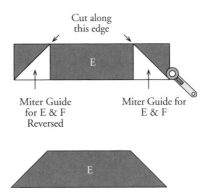

Figure 8.12

2. Sew the neutral and green Template B triangles together to make squares. Sew the light red-violet and the dark red-violet Template B triangles together to make squares.

3. Sew a dark red-violet Template B triangle to a neutral Template D rectangle. Repeat until four matching BD units are complete. Make four more BD units, reversing the direction of B. Sew a green C triangle to a blue-violet C triangle; repeat until four CC units are complete.(See Figure 8.13.)

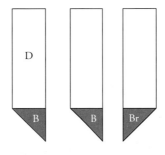

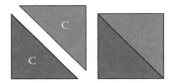

Figure 8.13

Block Size: 7½" (19 cm)

Setting: Four blocks, set on point

Fabric: 1½ yards (1½ meters) of gray-green neutral for background and border

1½ yards (1½ meters) of blue-violet for blocks, border, and binding

½ yard (½ meter) of red-violet for blocks and border

¾ yard (¾ meter) of green for blocks and border

⅛ yard (12 cm) of light red-violet for blocks

⅛ yard (12 cm) of a color between red-violet and blue-violet

⅛ yard (12 cm) of dark blue-violet

⅛ yard (12 cm) of neutral fabric overdyed in a light value of green

⅛ yard (12 cm) of green fabric overdyed in a light-to-medium value of blue-violet

Cutting: Template A: 4 neutral

Template B: 24 each neutral and green

20 each dark red-violet and light red-violet

8 dark blue-violet

Template C: 4 each neutral, blue-violet, and green

Template D: 8 neutral

(Cont. over)

Strip E: Four 3" x 16"
(7.6 cm x 40.6 cm)
red-violet

Strip F: Four 3" x 11¼"
(7.6 cm x 28.6 cm)
green

Template G: 4 neutral

Strip H: Eight 4" x 11¾"
(10.2 cm x 29.8 cm)
blue-violet

Template I: 8 green over-
dyed with blue-violet

Template J: 4 each from
fabric between blue-
violet and red-violet and
neutral overdyed in
green

Strip K: Eight 4" x 18¾"
(10.2 cm x 47.6 cm)
neutral. Cut ends for
mitered corners

Backing: 1 yard (1 meter)

4. Using Figure 8.14 as a guide, sew rows together as shown, taking care to place colors in the proper position. Make four basket blocks. Sew the basket blocks together.

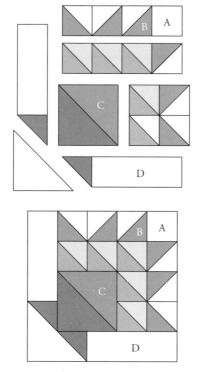

Figure 8.14

5. To make the inside borders, sew an E and an F strip together, then add a G triangle. Repeat for a total of four units. Sew one to each side of the basket unit. (See Figure 8.15.)

Figure 8.15

6. Look at Figure 8.16 to see how the interlocking and overlapping borders are pieced. For the outer borders, sew together a Strip K and a Strip H, repeating until you have eight HK units. Sew an I piece cut from the green overdyed in blue-violet to either side of a J piece cut from a color between blue-violet and red-violet. Select this color from a color run between blue and red. Sew another J piece in neutral overdyed with green to the top of the IJI piece. Make four of these IJIJ units. Complete the outer borders by sewing an HK unit to either side of an IJIJ unit, making one for each of the four sides of the quilt.

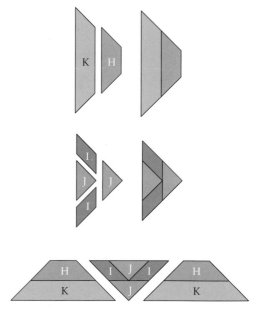

Figure 8.16

7. Sew the outer borders in place, matching all cross seams, and stitching to within ¼" (0.6 cm) of the edge. Fold the right sides together and stitch from the inside to the outside to complete the mitered corners.

8. Make a quilt sandwich of backing, batting, and quilt top; thread- or pin-baste. Quilt as desired. Bind and label.

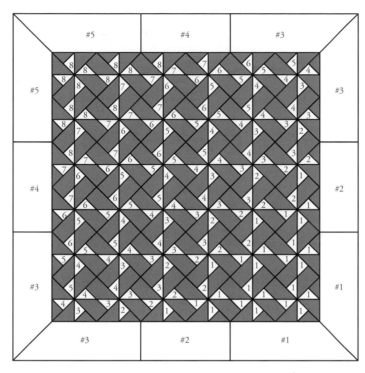

Figure 8.17

This glowing wall quilt is an example of what you can achieve with just two hues and the effective use of value. Eight even-step value gradations of terra cotta, arranged in a diagonal placement from light to dark, light up this quilt. Fabrics were dyed using the bowl and cup methods.

1. Make terra cotta blocks as listed below.

Terra Cotta Value	Number of Blocks
#1	3
#2	3
#3	4
#4	5
#5	4
#6	3
#7	2
#8	1

Begin by sewing a navy Template A to a terra cotta Template B triangle. Make four, then sew together as shown in Figure 8.18. Make a total of 25 blocks, and label each with the value number of the terra cotta.

Figure 8.18

Block size: 5¼" (13.3 cm)

Setting: 36 blocks, set 5 whole and 2 half-blocks by 5 whole and 2 half-blocks

Fabric: 1 yard (1 meter), cut into ⅛ yard (12 cm) pieces; dyed in 8 even-step gradations of terra cotta (bowl method) for blocks

1 yard (1 meter), cut into ⅛ yard (12 cm) pieces; dyed in 8 even-step gradations of terra cotta (cup method) for outer border

2 yards (1.8 meters), dyed navy blue for blocks, inner border, and binding (see Appendix 2)

Cutting: 100 of Template A in navy for blocks

44 each of Templates B and C in navy for borders

88 of Template B in terra cotta and 80 for borders as follows:

Value	Blocks	Inner Border
#1 (darkest)	12	13
#2	12	4
#3	16	4
#4	20	2
#5	16	4
#6	12	4
#7	8	4
#8 (lightest)	4	9

(Cont. over)

99

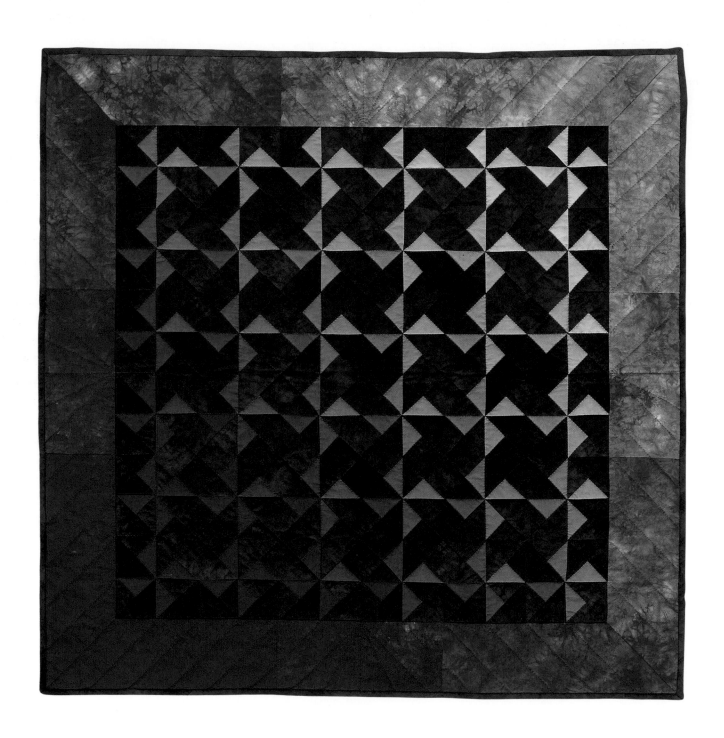

Hoptatopta
42½" x 42½" (108 cm x 108 cm)
Designed and machine-pieced by Cynthia Myerberg; hand-quilted by Delores Stemple, Aurora, WV
Eight even-step gradations of terra cotta light up this quilt. The warm/cool contrast of the
terra cotta against the navy blue plays visual tricks on the viewer.

2. For the inner pieced border, use the list below to determine how many squares of each value and type to make.

Terra Cotta Value	Block 2R	Block 2L
#1	6	7
#2	2	2
#3	2	2
#4	1	1
#5	2	2
#6	2	2
#7	2	2
#8	4	5

Begin by sewing a navy Template B triangle to a terra cotta Template B triangle. Sew each set of BB triangles to a navy Template C triangle. Note that some of the blocks require the navy triangle to be on the right (Block 2R); others require it on the left (Block 2L). (See Figure 8.19.) Label each finished border block with the value number of the terra cotta.

3. Use Figure 8.17 to piece together the blocks and borders. Begin by sewing the squares of the border into pairs as needed to begin and end each horizontal row of blocks. Take note of the way the two squares are placed together to get the correct color positioning. As you sew together each row, add the

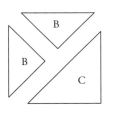

Block 2R   Block 2L

Figure 8.19

appropriate border units to the beginning and end of it. To finish the top and bottom rows of border blocks, sew them together as shown and attach them to the body of the quilt.

4. Using Figure 8.17 as a guide, place the outer borders. Sew the sections for each side together. Center the midsection of each border unit on one side of the quilt top. Stitch in place, beginning at the center and stopping ¼" (1.3 cm) from the outer edge. When all four border units are sewed on, miter the corners and trim away any excess fabric.

5. Make a quilt "sandwich" of backing, batting, and quilt top, and thread- or pin-baste in place. Quilt as desired. Bind and label.

For the outer borders, the sizes below in terra cotta.

Value	Quantity	Size
#1	2	5½" x 17" (13.9 cm x 43.1 cm)
#2	2	5½" x 11" (13.9 cm x 27.9 cm)
#3	4	5½" x 17" (13.9 cm x 43.1 cm)
#4	2	5½" x 11" (13.9 cm x 27.9 cm)
#5	2	5½" x 17" (13.9 cm x 43.1 cm)
Backing:		1¼ yards (1¼ meters)

THE RAINBOW MAKER
by Ashley Elizabeth Cohen, age 11

Up in the sky,
Over the trees,
In fluffy clouds
She feels a cool breeze.

She spins on her wheel.
She smiles at the sun.
She collects all the colors,
Because it's got to be done.

She's the Rainbow Maker,
Maker of dreams.
The smaller it is,
The bigger it seems.

She gathers the colors,
Red, yellow, and blue.
She makes millons of rainbows,
All just for you.

THE RAINBOW MAKER
43" x 43" (109 cm x 109 cm)
Designed and machine-pieced by Cynthia Myerberg; hand-quilted by Delores Stemple, Aurora, WV
Light- to medium-values of rainbow colors dyed by both the cup and bowl methods were used to
make this strip-pieced quilt.

Inspired by a poem by an 11-year-old poet, this quilt is made of light-to-medium values of fabrics from a rainbow-colored palette. This simple strip-pieced quilt can be made in a snap by even a beginning quilter. This version of the quilt uses fabrics from the various value workshops in *Dyeing to Quilt*; it would also be beautiful made from a color run between complementary colors.

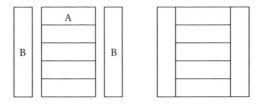

Figure 8.21

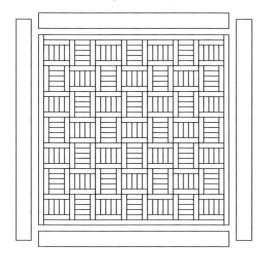

Figure 8.20

1. Rotary-cut the rainbow-colored fabrics into strips 1½" (3.8 cm) wide. Sew together lengthwise in groups of five.
2. From the strip-pieced groups, cut 49 sections that measure 3½" x 5½" (8.9 cm x 13.9 cm). From the medium-pink fabric, cut 98 strips that measure 1½" x 5½" (3.8 cm x 13.9 cm). Sew a pink strip to either side of a strip-pieced section, as shown in Figure 8.21.

3. Sew these blocks together in vertical rows of five. Then sew all rows together as in Figure 8.22.

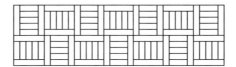

Figure 8.22

4. Cut two strips of blue for the inner border measuring 1½" x 35½" (3.8 cm x 90.1 cm). Sew them to opposite sides of the quilt top. Cut two more strips of blue, 1½" x 37½" (3.8 cm x 95.2 cm), and sew them to the two remaining sides of the quilt.
5. Cut two strips of pink for the outer border measuring 3½" x 37½" (8.9 cm x 45 cm). Sew them to opposite sides of the quilt top. Cut two more strips of pink 3½" x 43½" inches (8.9 cm x 110.4 cm), and sew them to the two remaining sides of the quilt.
6. Make a quilt sandwich of backing, batting, and top; thread- or pin-baste. Quilt as desired. Bind and label.

Block size: 5" (12.7 cm)

Setting: 49 blocks, set 7 by 7

Fabric: Assortment of ⅛ yard (12 cm) or ¼ yard (23 cm) fabrics in light-to-medium values of rainbow colors

½ yard (46 cm) pink

¼ yard (23 cm) medium-value blue for inner border

1 yard (1 meter) medium-value pink for outer border and binding

Backing: 1¼ yards (1¼ meters)

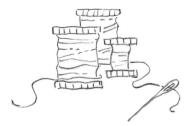

PLANNING A HAND-DYED QUILT

By now you have dyed quite a stash of fabrics and are surely brimming with ideas for quilt designs. Here are some general guidelines to planning successful quilts. Keep them in mind as you plan your new quilts using your hand-dyed fabrics.

- You must have some darks in your quilt to make your other colors look light. You can use a tool like the Ruby Beholder to determine the value of your fabrics. This is simply a piece of red plastic that serves to take color out of fabrics when you look at them through it. The fabrics appear light, medium, or dark in relation to each other.
- Because the eye goes toward the brightest, lightest colors, do not put them on the border or in the corners. That will take the focus away from the main body of the quilt and will cause a problem in keeping a focal point.

- Try to use a combination of shape, pattern, and color to produce a design for your quilt.
- Use the patterns of the mottled fabric and some of the new patterned fabrics you will create in Chapter Six to create visual interest on the surface of your quilt.
- To create depth and perspective in your quilt, use grays or neutrals with your other colors.
- Do not use complementary colors in equal proportions. Let one dominate the other.
- Try to create color harmony or unity in the quilt by spreading a color throughout different parts of the quilt.
- Consider a point of focus for the design, an area that is lighter or darker than the rest of the quilt. This could be in the center, off center, or in a corner.
- Coloration does not have to be uniform. It can move from dark to light across the quilt, horizontally, vertically, or diagonally.

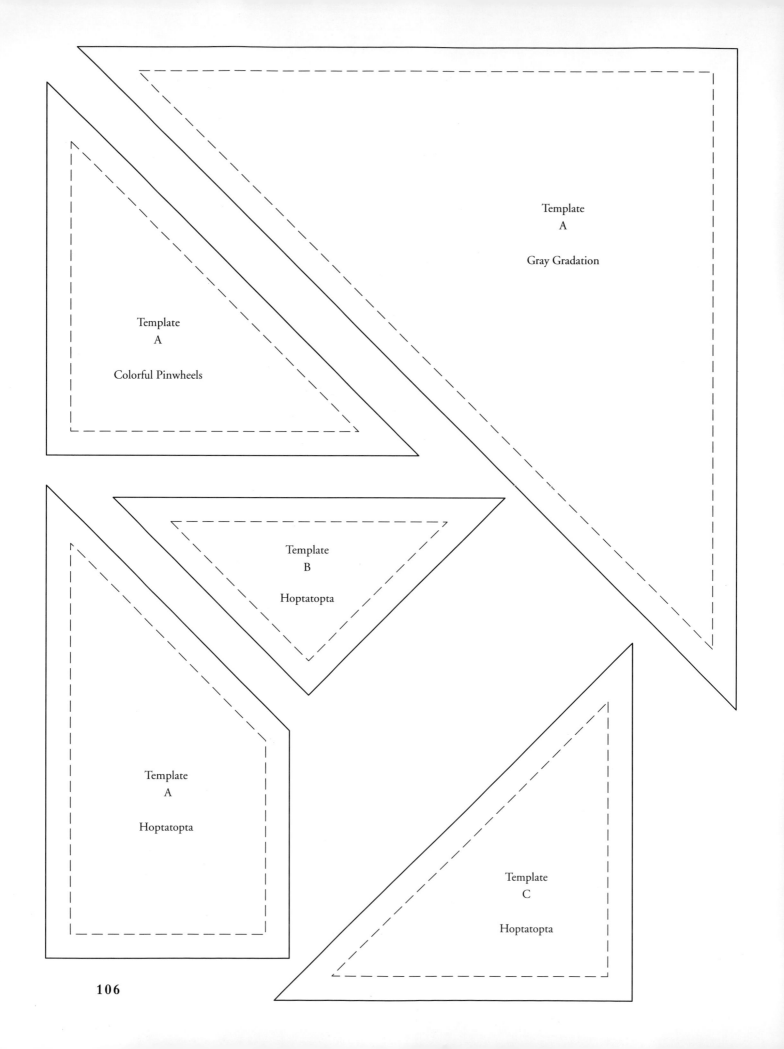

Template
A

Gray Gradation

Template
A

Colorful Pinwheels

Template
B

Hoptatopta

Template
A

Hoptatopta

Template
C

Hoptatopta

106

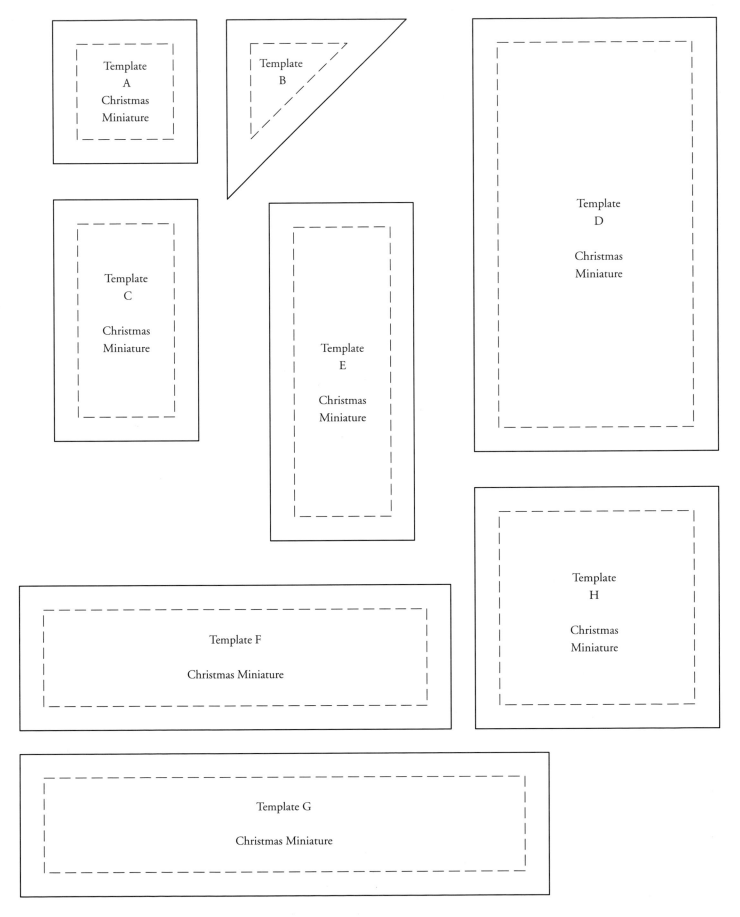

Template
A
Christmas
Miniature

Template
B

Template
D

Christmas
Miniature

Template
C

Christmas
Miniature

Template
E

Christmas
Miniature

Template
H

Christmas
Miniature

Template F

Christmas Miniature

Template G

Christmas Miniature

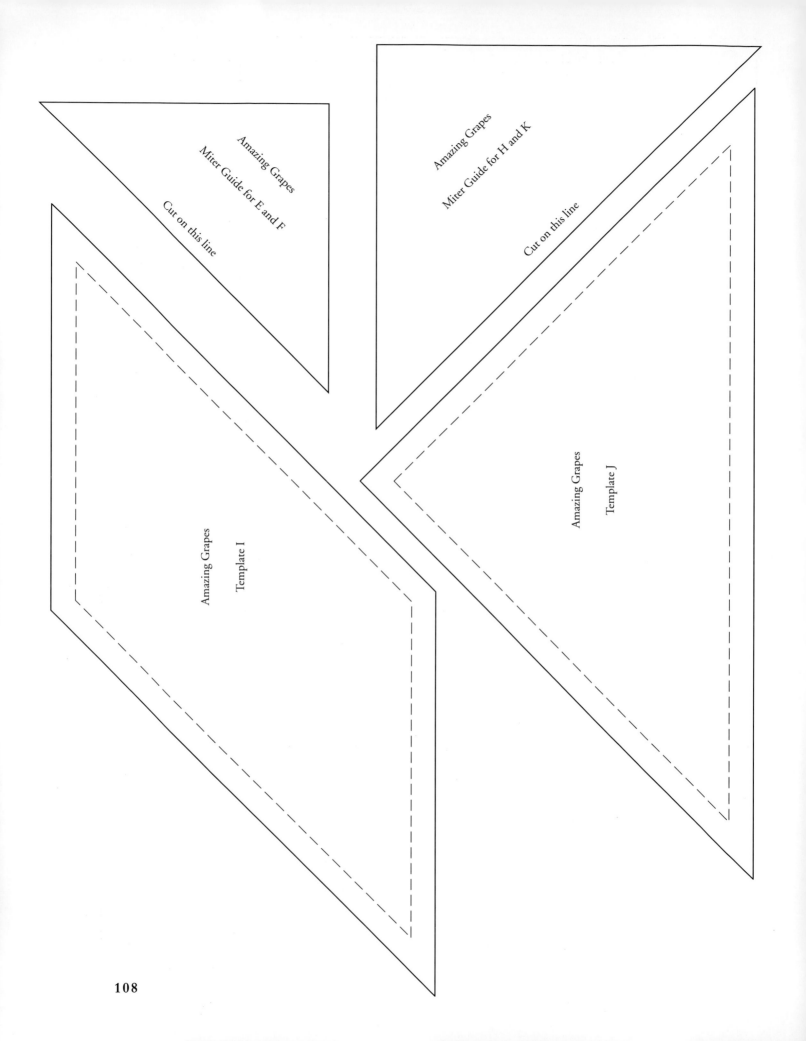

Amazing Grapes
Miter Guide for E and F

Cut on this line

Amazing Grapes
Miter Guide for H and K

Cut on this line

Amazing Grapes
Template I

Amazing Grapes
Template J

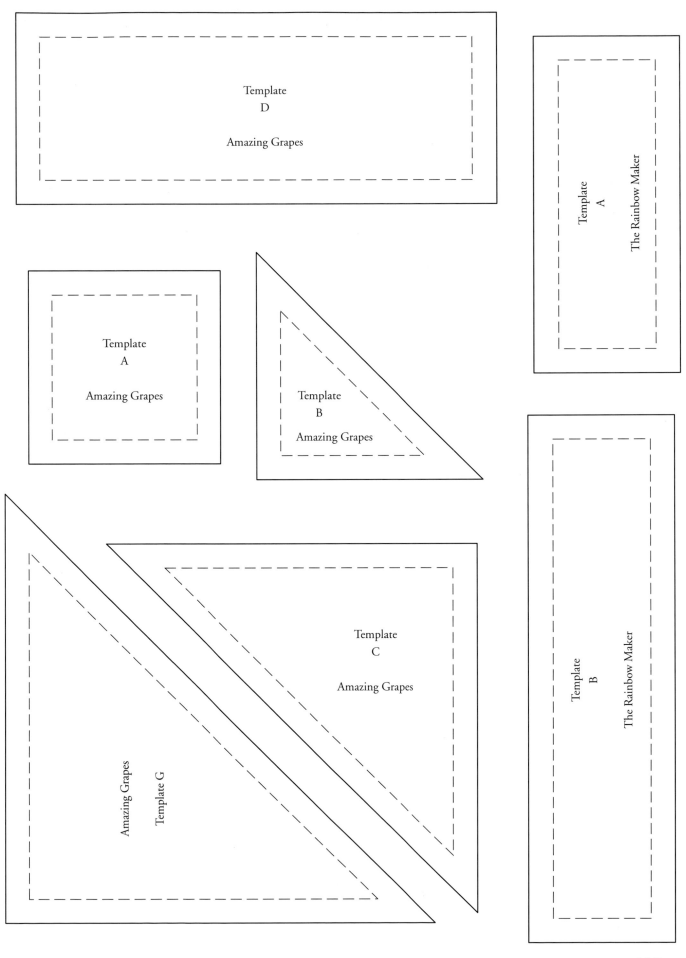

Template
D

Amazing Grapes

Template
A

The Rainbow Maker

Template
A

Amazing Grapes

Template
B

Amazing Grapes

Template
C

Amazing Grapes

Amazing Grapes
Template G

Template
B

The Rainbow Maker

Each of the three lesson plans provided is designed for a half-day session. All levels of students are encouraged, from beginner to advanced. The instructor should have on hand a selection of dye powders, a selection of pre-mixed dye solutions, and a selection of dyed fabrics.

LEARNING TO SEE COLOR

OBJECTIVES

Learn the cup and bowl methods of dyeing

Learn to mix dye solution (review safety considerations)

Learn to keep track of dyeing results

Learn the concept of primary and secondary colors

FABRIC

1½ yards (1¼ meters) per student

1. Demonstrate mixing dye solution. Have students mix their own solutions. Mix enough dye solution so that each student can dye 6 pieces of fabric.
2. Demonstrate dyeing one set of 6 pieces of fabric with the cup method and another set with the bowl method. Have students repeat the procedure. (Workshops 1.1 and 1.2.)
3. Using a pre-dyed set of 12 pieces of fabric, cut up into swatches and have students attach them to a record sheet. Discuss the leanings of each of the colors and those of any other samples available. Explain the concept of primary and secondary colors.
4. Explain how to cure hand-dyed fabrics. Have students take home their fabrics to cure, rinse, wash, dry, and iron.

OBJECTIVES

Learn how to alter color using one dye powder

Do an eight-step value gradation

Learn three ways of changing a color

FABRIC

3½ to 4 yards (3 to 3½ meters) per student

1. Demonstrate the mixing of dye solution and the measuring of dye solution.
2. Have students select a color to work with and complete each exercise after the teacher has demonstrated it:
   • An eight-step value gradation (see Workshop 4.2)
   • Changing the chroma of a color by adding black (see Workshop 4.3)
   • Changing a color by adding its complement (see page 48)
   • Changing a color by adding an analogous color (see page 47)
3. Discuss the results of each exercise, showing samples of pre-dyed fabrics. Show students how to keep track of results by using record sheets.
4. Explain how to cure hand-dyed fabrics. Have students take home their fabrics to cure, rinse, wash, dry, and iron.

DYEING A COLOR WHEEL

OBJECTIVES

Learn to make a simple 12-step color wheel

Learn about color wheels and color runs

Use both the cup and bowl methods

FABRIC

2 yards (1¾ meters) per student

1. Demonstrate the mixing of dye solution and the measuring of dye solution.

2. Use the three primaries, or help students select colors to work with. Demonstrate how to create a 12-step color wheel and have students work on their own wheels (see Workshop 2.1). Have half the students use the cup method and half the students use the bowl method. Compare the results.

3. Using pre-dyed samples, discuss the colors created. Explain how to expand the color wheel into a 27-step color run (see Workshop 3.1).

4. Using left-over dye solution, have students experiment to create light values of randomly mixed colors (see Workshop 7.2).

5. Show students how to keep track of results by using record sheets.

6. Explain how to cure hand-dyed fabrics. Have students take home their fabrics to cure, rinse, wash, dry, and iron.

DYEING FABRICS TO MAKE A SMALL QUILT

OBJECTIVES

Use the cup method of dyeing

Learn to dye for a specific quilt project

Produce a variety of hand-dyed fabrics

FABRIC

2¼ yards (2 meters)

1. Discuss the type of quilt students wish to make. The simple quilts on pages 92 and 95 are good for this exercise. Discuss color use across the quilt.

2. Have students select dye powders. Suggest using two primaries, two complements, or two analogous colors. Show samples fabrics.

3. Demonstrate how to mix dye solution and have students mix their own.

4. Review the cup method and have students dye fabrics (see Workshop 1.2).

5. Show students how to keep track of results by using record sheets.

6. Explain how to cure hand-dyed fabrics. Have students take home their fabrics to cure, rinse, wash, dry, and iron.

7. Have students make their quilts from the dyed fabrics. Try to have the class meet again to compare quilts.

RECORD SHEET #1: COLOR TEST RESULTS

Attach your swatches to the chart and record details of the Workshop below.

Workshop: _____

Dye Method: _____

Dye Solution: _____

Color(s): _____

Notes: _____

_____

_____

Fabric #1

Fabric #6

Fabric #2

Fabric #5

Fabric #4

Fabric #3

Attach your swatches to the wheel and record the formulas beside them.

Workshop: _____

Dye Method: _____

Dye Solutions: _____

Color(s):

  Red: _____

  Yellow: _____

  Blue: _____

Notes: _____

_____

_____

RECORD SHEET #3: 27 COLOR RUN RESULTS

Row 1

A 4T	3T + 2½tsp	3T + 1tsp	2T + 2tsp	2T	1T + 1tsp	2tsp	½tsp	0
B 0	½tsp	2tsp	1T + 1tsp	2T	2T + 2tsp	3T + 1tsp	3T + 2½tsp	4T

Row 2

A 4T	3T + 2½tsp	3T + 1tsp	2T + 2tsp	2T	1T + 1tsp	2tsp	½tsp	0
B 0	½tsp	2tsp	1T + 1tsp	2T	2T + 2tsp	3T + 1tsp	3T + 2½tsp	4T

Row 3

A 4T	3T + 2½tsp	3T + 1tsp	2T + 2tsp	2T	1T + 1tsp	2tsp	½tsp	0
B 0	½tsp	2tsp	1T + 1tsp	2T	2T + 2tsp	3T + 1tsp	3T + 2½tsp	4T

Workshop: _____

Attach your swatches to the large rectangles and record the mixing formula for each.

Row 1
Dye Method: _____
Dye Solution: _____
Color(s): _____
Notes: _____

Row 2
Dye Method: _____
Dye Solution: _____
Color(s): _____
Notes: _____

Row 3
Dye Method: _____
Dye Solution: _____
Color(s): _____
Notes: _____

T=tablespoon
tsp=teaspoon

Workshop: _____

Attach your swatches to the
large squares and record the
mixing formula for each.

Dye Method: _____

Dye Solution: _____

Color(s): _____

Notes: _____
_____
_____
_____

FORMULAS FOR DYEING LARGE PIECES OF FABRIC

Solutions may be used full strength or diluted.

FABRIC	DYE SOLUTION	CONTAINER SIZE	METHOD
¼ yard/meter	½ cup (4 oz)	10 or 12 oz	Bowl or cup
½ yard/meter	¾ cup (6 oz)	16 oz	Bowl or cup
1 yard/meter	1 cup (8 oz)	32 oz	Cup
1½ yards/meters	1½ cups (12 oz)	32 oz	Cup
2 yards/meters	2 cups (16 oz)	64 oz	Cup

APPENDIX 3
NON-MIXED DYE COLORS

The Workshops in *Dyeing to Quilt* use the following dyes. Non-mixed colors usually have a color index (CI) number; mixed colors do not.

MX DESIGNATION	CI NUMBER	PRO	DHARMA
Yellow MX-3RA	FR Orange 86	Golden Yellow 104	Deep Yellow #4
Yellow MX-8G	FR Yellow 86	Sun Yellow 108	Lemon Yellow #1
Yellow MX-GR	FR-Yellow 7	Tangerine Yellow 112	Golden Yellow #3
Yellow MX-4G	FR Yellow 22	Lemon Yellow 114	
Orange MX-2R	FR Orange 2	Strong Orange 202	Deep Orange #6
Red MX-8B	FR Red 11	Fuchsia 308	Fuchsia Red #13
Red MX-5B	FR Red 2	Mixing Red 305	Light Red #12
Red MX-6BDA	FR Brown 40	Burgundy 316	
Blue MX-R	FR Blue 4	Basic Blue 400	Sky Blue #26
Blue MX-2G 125	FR Blue 109	Mixing Blue 402	Cobalt Blue #22
Blue MX-G Conc.	FR Blue 163	Intense Blue 406	Cerulean Blue #33
Turquoise MX-G	FR Blue 140	Turquoise 410	Turquoise #25
Brown MX-5BR	FR Brown 10	Red Brown 505	Maroon Brown #36

MIXED DYES USED IN *DYEING TO QUILT*

MX DESIGNATION	CI NUMBER	PRO	DHARMA
MX-GBA		Red 312	Chinese Red #10A
MX-BRA		Scarlet 300	Scarlet #9
MX-CBA		Green 700	
MX-CWA		Black 608	
MX-CWNA			New Black
MX-CRA		Brown 510	

APPENDIX 4
MIXING FORMULAS FOR TWO-COLOR DYE RUNS

Use these charts to mix quantities of dye solution for the nine gradations in a two-color dye run.

Use this chart to make ½ cup (4 oz) dye solution to dye fat quarters of fabric--18"x 22" (46 cm x 56 cm)--instead of fat eighths--11" x 18" (28 cm x 46 cm). Use these for a color dye run or use the chart below to select any single cup number (a specific color) and make an eight even-step gradation (see Workshop 4.2).

Cup #1
½ cup of Color A

Cup #2
7 tablespoons + 2 teaspoons of Color A
1 teaspoon of Color B

Cup #3
6 tablespoons + 2 teaspoons of Color A
1 tablespoon + 1 teaspoon of Color B

Cup #4
5 tablespoons + 1 teaspoon of Color A
2 tablespoons + 2 teaspoons of Color B

Cup #5
4 tablespoons of Color A
4 tablespoons of Color B

Cup #6
2 tablespoons + 2 teaspoons of Color A
5 tablespoons + 1 teaspoon of Color B

Cup #7
1 tablespoon + 1 teaspoon of Color A
6 tablespoons + 2 teaspoons of Color B

Cup #8
1 teaspoon of Color A
7 tablespoons + 2 teaspoons of Color B

Cup #9
½ cup of Color B

These are the same formulas as the previous set, but they give you 1 cup (8 oz) dye solution instead of ½ cup (4 oz). Use this chart to select any single cup number (a specific color) to use as Color A or Color B in a nine-step dye run. You can also use the chart to dye 1 ½ yards (meters) of fabric.

Cup #1
1½ cups of Color A

Cup #2
1¼ cups + 3 tablespoons of Color A
1 tablespoon of Color B

Cup #3
1¼ cups of Color A
¼ cup of Color B

Cup #4
1 cup of Color A
½ cup of Color B

Cup #5
¾ cup of Color A
¾ cup of Color B

Cup #6
½ cup of Color A
1 cup of Color B

Cup #7
¼ cup of Color A
1¼ cups of Color B

Cup #8
1 tablespoon of Color A
1¼ cups + 3 tablespoons of Color B

Cup #9
1½ cups of Color B

APPENDIX 5
EQUIVALENCY CHARTS

1 tablespoon = 3 teaspoons = 1/2 oz = 1/16 cup

1 oz = 2 tablespoons = 1/8 cup = 6 teaspoons

1 cup = 8 oz = 16 tablespoons = 48 teaspoons

1 teaspoon = 1/3 tablespoon = 1/6 oz = 1/48 cup

1 inch = 2.54 cm

⅛ yard, selvage to selvage = 11.4 cm x 114 cm

¼ yard, selvage to selvage = 22.9 cm x 114 cm

½ yard, selvage to selvage = 45.7 cm x 114 cm

¾ yard, selvage to selvage = 68.9 cm x 114 cm

1 yard, selvage to selvage = 36" x 45" = 91 cm x 114 cm

Fat quarter = 18" x 22"= 46 cm x 56 cm

Fat eighth = 11" x 18" = 28 cm x 46 cm

To convert Centigrade to Fahrenheit:

      Multiply C by 9

      Divide by 5

      Add 32

To convert Fahrenheit to Centigrade:

      Subtract 32 from F

      Multiply by 5

      Divide by 9

ALJO Manufacturing Company
81 Franklin Street
New York, NY 10013

Colorado Wholesale Dye Corporation
2139 S. Sheridan Boulevard
Denver, CO 80227

Dharma Trading Company
PO Box 150916
San Rafael, CA 94915

Dick Blick Art Materials
PO Box 1267
Galesburg, IL 61402-1267

Earth Guild
33 Haywood Street, Department FA
Asheville, NC 28801

Lunn Fabrics
357 North Santa Fe Drive
Denver, CO 80223

PRO Chemical and Dye, Inc.
PO Box 14
Somerset, MA 20726

Rupert, Gibbon, and Spider, Inc.
PO Box 425
Healdsburg, CA 95448

Testfabrics, Inc.
PO Box 420
Middlesex, NJ 08846

BIBLIOGRAPHY

DYEING FABRIC

Blumenthal, Betsy and Kathryn Kreider, *Hands On Dyeing*, Interweave Press (1988)
De Boer, Janet, Editor, *Dyeing for Fibres and Fabrics*, Kangaroo Press (1987)
Dryden, Deborah, *Fabric Painting and Dyeing for the Theatre*, Heinemann Publishing (1993)
Johnston, Ann, *Dye Painting*, American Quilter's Society (1992)
Knutson, Linda, *Synthetic Dyes for Natural Fibers*, Interweave Press, 1986
Milner, Ann, *The Ashford Book of Dyeing*, Bridget Williams Books Limited (1992)
Tescher, Judy Mercer, *Dyeing and Overdyeing of Cotton Fabrics*, American Quilter's Society (1990)
Walter, Judy Anne, *A Dyers Handbook*, Cooler by the Lake Publications (1989)
Widger, Katy J., *Color Wheel Dyeing for Quilters*, Katy J. Widger (1992)

COLOR THEORY FOR QUILTERS

Beyer, Jinny, *Color Confidence for Quilters*, The Quilt Digest Press (1992)
Itten, Johannes, *The Elements of Color*, Van Nostrand Reinhold Co. (1970)
McKelvey, Susan Richardson, *Color for Quilters*, A Yours Truly Publication (1984)
McKelvey, Susan Richardson, *Light and Shadows*, C&T Publishing (1989)
Penders, Mary Coyne, *Color and Cloth*, The Quilt Digest Press (1989)
Wilcox, Michael, *Blue and Yellow Don't Make Green*, North Light Books (1994)
Wolfrom, Joen, *The Magical Effects of Color*, C&T Publishing (1992)